Down the Up Staircase

The Way Up is Down

Sheila Parnell

Published by:
Benchmark Basic Media
PO Box 1185
The Dalles, Oregon 97058
www.bbasicmedia.com

Cover Design: Sheila Parnell
Cover Photo: Stacey Dixon

.   ISBN: 0996704000
ISBN-13: 9780996704007

DEDICATION

I dedicate this book to my exceptional husband, Phil Parnell. You have endured my journey "lower" into Christ Jesus. You walked with me while I learned to lay down my pride and self-will, which at times made it very interesting for you. Thank you for your encouragement and your enduring faithfulness.

Also, I dedicate this book to the many people who are searching to find their purpose in life. May this book further you in your search of God and your life's role apart from religious practices of performance. Be free to be!

CONTENTS

ACKNOWLEDGMENTS

I want to thank Terry Murphy and Word Weavers for your critique of my writing which helped me tremendously as I continue to learn how to hone my writing skills. You helped to begin to draw out of me what was hidden away.

Thank you to Fred Blakely for editing this book and for all your encouragement to get it published. May your book follow soon.

Thank you Steve and Leslie for your help in editing.

Thank you Stacey Dixon for your encouragement over the years and for the perfect photo you took, while in Israel, for the cover of this book. The trouble it took for you to snap that shot is so appreciated!

Also, I want to thank my countless friends, too many to name, who have supported me all these years as I have endeavored to learn how to step into God's destiny for me. May you run free in yours.

Last but, definitely, not least I want to thank God for His speaking prophetically through people about my writing. Without that I would have never written anything. Of course You knew that! Thank you for the awesome journey of knowing You more and more in intimacy. I'm excited about what the future holds and what greater revelation awaits for Your timed release. I love your Goodness.

1 The Dream

The dream played out before me as if it were really happening. The scenes were very vivid and I could feel the emotion of the dream. This dream sent me on a journey searching for its hidden meaning. Along this journey God gave additional revelation to the dream which has changed my life forever. This book is what I discovered along the way.

"I was in a car driving in the countryside on a highway. I had the strong impression I had been to my destination before. Glancing down at the speedometer I saw I was going 90 miles an hour. Immediately I slowed down. As I entered a town I was glancing around trying to remember where my destination was. The roads were narrow with rock walls on both sides.

The scene immediately changed to where I was walking down what seemed like a sidewalk with a concrete wall to my left. All the while I was trying to remember how to get to the place where I was going.

As I was walking down the walkway I came to an opening to the left and I went through it. Around the corner there were two carpeted stairways; one was going up and the other was going down. I had the impression that the stairway going down was the correct choice. As I began my descent, the steps began moving upward in the opposite direction much like an escalator. The steps became narrow and were moving very fast so I had to move my feet quickly so I would not fall. There was no frustration or the feeling I was going the wrong direction.

Ahead of me there was a woman also going down the stairs. She was laughing as she moved quickly to navigate the moving stairs. She yelled at me "Just move really fast!"

I had to be careful how I put my foot on the narrow steps. I came to a landing and then continued forward onto the next set of moving stairs. There were three sets of stairs with landings between them.

In the shadows further ahead I could see other people. Close to the bottom there was the silhouette of a woman falling as she descended the steps. I gasped feeling sorry for her as she struggled to get back up. The people faded out of the picture and I did not see what happened to the woman from that point.

Then I came to the bottom of the landing where my downward momentum propelled me to the right. It was like I had no control of my movements. My descent was powerfully pushing me forward. To my surprise I was thrust onto a slide that swiftly delivered me into a deep pool of water.

As I was treading the bottomless pool I looked up at the building I had come out of. On the second floor I saw a glass walled room. Inside the room was a group of people looking towards the windowed wall. Some were sitting and some were standing. I sensed the woman who had descended the stairs with me was now in the water next to me. But yet I could not see her.

Looking at the room I realized this was the place I was looking for. I had found my destination. Turning away from the room I began to swim to the edge of the pool.

There seemed to be an urgency for me to get out of the water before anyone saw me. As I was crawling out of the water the people in the room began to move toward the window to watch me. The dream ended."

The way up is down. The kingdom of God is opposite from man's thinking. While God beckons us to go higher our usual response is an attempt to go up through our own effort. But God's higher path can only be found by going lower.

Many people strive to go up the ladder of success. Many vie for a position by scrambling for recognition. Often this involves climbing over others to be first. This is true for most of the world and sad to say, also of many Christians. The stairway leading "up" is a wide, effortless path. In fact it doesn't take much effort going that way; it's an easy road to travel. It is a natural path for man's fleshly nature.

Jesus taught about how entering through the narrow gate leads to life instead of the wide gate that leads to ruin or loss. (Matt 7:13,14). Many choose the wide gate; the automatic stairs moving upward toward human elevation often ending in man's downfall. It is an effortless pursuit we have all at some time or another participated in.

The narrow gate is represented by descending the stairs while they are moving upward. Going through the narrow gate is by not allowing the upward movement of the stairs to keep us from going lower. The way up is running opposite from the self-directing nature humans tend to choose. Too often it is easier to ride the always upward moving stairs than to choose to go lower by laying down our own wisdom to become selfless. But, truthfully we often don't know how to find that narrow gate because we are unaware of how often we do live according to our own fleshly wisdom or self-sufficiency.

In looking at Jesus' life we can see His definite descent down the up staircase. He did not please Himself. He could have chosen to live from His already elevated position as God. But yet, He chose to go lower and live in the form of fallen man by choosing to only please the Father in every way. This is truthfully how He overcame the flesh to the point of dying a horrible death on the cross; going lower to gain life for all. It was only by accomplishing the "lower" that qualified Him to rise up into the "higher", seated beside God as the conquering

Lion of Judah! He would not have overcome death if he had not first descended lower. (Phil 2:5-9).

Jesus did not show us what He could do as God. He showed us how He, as a man, overcame sin. He basically showed us what we can do to overcome…it is possible. To function as an overcomer all depends upon learning to go lower; by laying down our self-will and our own wisdom just as Jesus did.

One time I had a vision of a room with a lot of boxes scattered all around on the floor. From somewhere I could hear someone knocking. There were no doors in the room. I began moving the boxes from the middle of the floor. Clearing the floor I found a door in the floor of the room. The knocking was coming from there. When I opened the door Jesus was standing there tirelessly knocking; He was waiting for me to find the door under all my boxes of self-effort.

Revelation 3:20-21 speak of Jesus standing at the door knocking. While knocking He waited for someone to hear Him, find the door and let Him in. Those who find the door and invite Him in are overcomers. What did they overcome? The same fleshly tendency Jesus overcame.

After we go lower He then raises us up to be seated with Him beside the Father. The way down truly is the way up.

What God showed me is that when we move the boxes of self-sufficiency and fleshly actions we will be able to find the door in the floor. We can't open the door until we bend down lower, grab the handle and open it. By attentively listening to Jesus' knock we can know the path to follow and what needs to be removed to give Him rule in our lives. The way to live a victorious life is to go lower; laying down our way and moving into Jesus' way. The way up is down.

Let's take a journey into the discovery of the way "down" so we can be lifted "up" by Jesus.

Down the Up Staircase

2 The Fall

Tilted Truth

Adam and Eve found themselves drawn into a discussion with the serpent about what God said about the tree of knowledge. The serpent's words were laced with a devastating tilt of God's truth. His words held just enough truth to be convincing. Each word was crafted to provoke Adam and Eve to question God in hopes to tilt them away from their trusted position in God. What was the conversation which wreaked so much destruction? It affected all of creation.

"And he said to the woman, Can it really be that God has said, you shall not eat from every tree of the garden? You shall not surely die." (Gen 3:1). As Adam and Eve entertained the question, suspicion made them wonder if God was withholding something from them. Insecurity began to develop foreign thoughts and feelings within them. Were they really safe with what God had been telling them?

The serpent continued, "For God knows that in the day you eat of it your eyes will be opened and you will be like God, knowing the difference between good and evil and blessing and calamity." (Gen 3:5).

More questions raced through their minds, *But, we thought we were already created in God's image? Is there something missing in us that God is not telling us?* They found themselves feeling less than who God had said they were. Was He withholding information from them about their identity? Inferiority began to restructure their perception of who they were. Doubt began to tilt them away from the truth and their identity.

Satan's words were true enough in part. There was just enough of God's truth to make it believable. They failed to understand the words were tilted and they began to question their Maker. Satan's strategy at that time is still his strategy today; it hasn't changed throughout the history of the earth. In the same way these tactics are unleashed upon us causing us to question God through our reasoning of what we think is truth. Just like Adam and Eve, we too try to deal with what we think is missing within us through our own strength. We mistakenly provide a false solution by taking matters into our own hands thus excluding God from the process.

There was a time I felt I had gained too much weight (somewhat menial compared to what is going on in the world, but it makes my point). Having always been thin I never had to worry about weight so I had developed an idea of what I thought I should look like. After giving birth to five children I no longer weighed the same as in my younger years, I believed I was overweight. But when I entered menopause my metabolism slowed down and for the first time I knew what overweight was; it left me longing to fit into those pants I once thought were too big. I had a wrong perception about my weight. If I had not operated out of my skewed view of my body then my awareness would have been much different. The truth was that I had gained weight, but my own perception tilted the truth of what I actually looked like. What I perceived as truth was only a tilted truth. How often do we miss what is really going on because we think we hold all the truth according to our own understanding?

A car swerved suddenly into my lane sending my foot slamming down onto the brake. "What is their problem?" I muttered. I effortlessly formed my own opinion about the person and what happened. Hidden from my understanding was that their hot coffee broke free from the cup holder scalding their leg. My own judgment made them out to be a dimwit who couldn't drive! Even though it was unsafe it was not intentional; we all make similar mistakes. My point of view was incomplete truth. The whole truth was blocked from my understanding. I judged them from my own limited perception which is tilted truth.

Satan's most effective tool used against mankind is to isolate people from their God given identity through insecurity and inferiority. It is very effective. Gideon is a prime example of this.

There was a faint breeze pushing past Gideon's face as he gazed into the starry sky. His thoughts dwelt on the dream he had overheard the Midianite tell his companions. The dream clearly told of Gideon's victory. He could still feel the wave of dismay that shot through him as the words reached his ears. A tingle of excitement rose within him as the words took his breath away. God had given him another sure sign that with only 300 men God would give him the victory over the Midianites. Not many hours prior he was living life as usual; in despair, working to find food for their next meal.

It had now been seven years since the Midianites and the Amalekites had begun to devastate the land by swarming in by the thousands. As they moved throughout the land they destroyed the crops and cattle until all was gone. The lack of sustenance and constant abuse caused them to hide in fear. The people had resorted to extreme measures to stay alive.

Gideon raced down the path pressing closely to the rock wall. While dodging the dangling branches his eyes probed the area for anyone watching. He halted, catching his breath at the sharp noise piercing the air. His head jerked toward the sound as he caught sight of a deer vaulting from behind a bush. With a forced release of his breath he continued down the path as his heart pounded in his chest. He must quickly finish threshing the wheat before anyone finds his reserve.

As he descended through the entrance of the winepress he could finally slow down. His hair clung to his sweaty brow. The breeze felt good as it swept over his face.

Walking down to the vat he removed the wood that hid what few wheat shafts were left. He pulled the shafts onto the treading platform and began to beat them with the flail. As he worked he could hear the wind rustling through the oak leaves that hung over the winepress providing a needed shade from the sun. There were no grapes to harvest; they had all been destroyed so the winepress became his hidden workplace.

'Gideon," a voice broke through Gideon's thoughts which caused him to jump. His jaw dropped as he looked up at a large man glowing with light standing under the oak tree on the edge of the rock wall. "The Lord is with you, you mighty man of courage," the stranger continued.

In disbelief Gideon shot back resentfully, "Sir, if the Lord is with us, then why has all this been happening to us? And where are all His wondrous works that our fathers told us about when the Lord brought us up from Egypt? But now the Lord has forsaken us and given us into the hand of Midianites."

The man leaned toward him and spoke purposefully, "Go in this your might, and you shall save Israel from the hand of Midian. Have I not sent you?"

Gideon thought, *This guy doesn't understand the situation we are in*. A sneering laugh escaped Gideon's mouth as he said, "How can I deliver Israel? My clan is the poorest in Manasseh and I am of no importance in my father's house."

A smile tugged at the corner of the man's mouth as he said, "Surely I will be with you and you shall smite the Midianites as one man."

All Gideon could think was, *Right! This guy doesn't know who he is talking to*. Then Gideon had an idea. He said to the man, "If now I have found favor in your sight, then show me a sign that it is God who is talking to me through you. Do not leave here, please, until I come back to you and bring my offering and set it down before you."

The man agreed, "I will wait for you to return."

Gideon would never forget the event to follow as he placed his offering of meat and bread before the man. The man raised his staff and touched the offering and it immediately caught fire and was consumed. The man quickly disappeared and Gideon knew he had been talking to an angel of God.

That memory and the other signs God had given blanketed him warmly with courage to stand on the outskirts of the Midianites camp surrounding them in the middle of the night with only 300 men. All insecurity was gone; he now trusted what God said. With a torch and clay pot in each of the men's left hand and a trumpet in their right hand the men watched and waited for his signal. How could this be? He was the least in his family, but yet God had called him mighty. God had seen what Gideon could not see in himself.

Gideon raised his trumpet to his mouth and blew with all his might. The sound of 300 trumpets blowing at once sent shivers up and down his spine. The air was electrified with the unified breaking of clay jars followed by the light of torches piercing the darkness. All at once every man screamed deafeningly, "The sword for the Lord and for Gideon!" Dead silence weighed heavily in the air. The hush was shredded by shrieks of terror from the Midianite camp as thousands began to flee sending tremors throughout the land at their departure. (Judges 6).

The truth of Gideon's situation was continuous harassment and starvation, but his limited perception blinded by bitterness and insecurity tilted the whole truth.

He could not see that God was bigger than their circumstance. God had to confront Gideon's limited understanding to align him with the truth that God had made him mighty. Once Gideon began to accept God's truth about himself nothing was going to stop him. Like Gideon, what tilted truths are we believing? How are these misaligned truths keeping us from living as God sees us? Truth from our own understanding causes us to miss the mark of our destiny here on earth.

Tilted truth comes in subtle ways to keep us from connecting with our true identity. One misaligned truth is that man's created purpose is to worship God. Sounds noble, but is that true? When this teaching was first released it did bring many into a deeper place of worship. But yet it has silently kept us inches away from our true purpose; tilted from the truth. Mankind was created for so much more…relationship. Out of all creation Adam and Eve were the only ones walking and conversing with God in the garden, created in His image. They were created for relationship. Then from relationship worship flowed naturally out of them. Worship was a product of their relationship not their purpose of existence. It is a truth tilted out of alignment with God's truth.

The truth is mankind was commissioned to govern the earth with authority. They were the dads of the earth filling it with heaven. We get derailed by thinking our purpose on earth is to die and go to heaven. Longing to vacate this earth derails us from our identity as governors. We spend our time thinking we have arrived when we accept Jesus as our savior. Jesus did not save us to go to heaven; he saved us to bring heaven to earth. Not understanding our purpose keeps us from moving into our true mandate to govern the earth, reconciling it to God and bringing heaven to earth.

It is our own wisdom and understanding that tilts God's truth out of alignment. It is kind of like someone standing on a balance beam and then someone puts a 20 pound weight into one of their hands. The weight will throw them off balance which can cause them to fall off the beam. Likewise our own understanding, as extra weight, throws us off balance from God's truth.

When we begin to see that we have a limited understanding then we can come into conformity with God's truth. It will bring us into union with what God says and we will no longer live according to the limitation of our own understanding. We will no longer be tilted away from God's truth but securely aligned in Him.

It's time to lean into the fullness of God's promises and purposes where we live from His vantage point. The way up to God is to go lower by laying down our own understanding.

The Trust Factor

Before the fall Adam and Eve had full trust in God; it was all they knew. After all He completed them and there was nothing missing from their life. Trust was not even a question until their lethal conversation with the serpent. Trust then became a factor.

Questions and doubt overrode their normal existence. Trust was sabotaged isolating them from their creator. When trust was gone all creation became separated in itself. Mankind was now isolated in the limitation of his own wisdom and judgment. Trust became a foreign way of life on earth.

Trust is *to have or place reliance; to depend on someone or something.* Adam and Eve's dependence shifted from God unto themselves as the "all knowing ones." Mankind from that point on would lean upon their own understanding. Trusting others became a very difficult thing for the earth's entire history.

A few years ago I was flying back home from England. Having found my seat I sat watching as others boarded. It interested me how hundreds of people could brush past one another, shoulder to shoulder, but yet were completely preoccupied with what they were doing. Some were stowing luggage away, others had to patiently and impatiently wait, and some were fussing with their belt and pillow. It was like they were in their own little world mostly oblivious of anyone else.

Then Holy Spirit gave me a picture of creation before the fall. All of life existed as one connected sphere. Everything was in unison, kind of like one large bubble. When Adam and Eve ate from the tree of knowledge they became self-focused instead of God-focused. From that point on their trust in what God said transferred to their judgment of right and wrong. With this shift all of creation collapsed into individual isolated bubbles - creation wasn't in unison anymore. This same disconnect has allocated us into an isolated existence. We can be in the midst of many people, but yet confined to our own little world - isolated in self.

We can see this even in the animals. They are very self-focused.

Our dog, Sebastian, is a prime example. The pleading big brown eyes stared at me as the wet black nose bore its way onto my lap. His hundred ten pound bull mastiff body moved like an accordion propelled by the rapid movement of his tail. The large paw found its way onto my knee as he began to shift himself forward onto my lap. He had no clue as to how big he really was; all he knew was that he wanted to snuggle. Snuggle is a big stretch of the word when considering the gigantic bony body wanting to get close! Even after all the repeated rejections he still tried. Though He does get his snuggle from time to time when my son is willing to allow the big guy to sit and sleep with him.

At one point I thought he might not be getting enough attention so I began to pour affection on him as much as possible. He enjoyed it greatly, but I found there was never enough; he even began to demand more of my time. So much for more attention! I get the distinct feeling that he thinks I was put on planet earth just for him; feed me, pet me and snuggle with me. He is very self-focused...but most animals are.

At one time the animals lived in harmony with all of creation before they became isolated in distrust. This is why all of creation is groaning for the sons of God to be revealed; it longs for selfishness to cease. Creation feels the pain of isolation. It longs to be reconnected once again in trust.

The tree of knowledge played a greater role in our connection to God than we realize. Many of us don't understand why the tree was in the garden to begin with and many even believe it was a bad tree. Yet, after God created everything He called it all good. So that means all the trees in the garden were good; even the tree of knowledge of good and evil. How could the tree of knowledge be good? Wasn't it the cause of the fall of man?

As I wondered about the tree of knowledge I began to study what evil means. I have discovered it is that which is not of God. The Ancient Hebrew Research Center

Mechanical Translation defines *good* as *function* and *evil* as *dysfunction*. From that understanding we can get a better idea that the tree of knowledge was about function and dysfunction. All knowledge was in God and all Adam and Eve had to do was to rest in that assurance - they didn't have to worry about right and wrong. When Adam and Eve ate of the tree they moved from functioning in their unity with God and became dysfunctional in the isolation of self-focus.

I was intrigued with the idea that the tree of knowledge was completely good so I began to ask God what was the purpose of the tree and why not to eat of it? I pondered it for a few months and then during one of my quiet times God showed me something I did not expect.

While house sitting for a friend, my everyday distractions faded in the shadows as I sat in the rocker letting the worship music wash over me. I could feel the movement of Holy Spirit warmly sweeping through me. There is nothing as sweet as interacting with the Spirit of God. My thoughts wandered onto the tree of knowledge and its purpose. Suddenly a picture flashed before me. I saw a piece of upholstered material with a tack holding it onto a section of wood. Then the tack came out and the fabric fell away from the wood.

As I pondered what I saw I realized it represented the tree of knowledge. The tree like the tack anchored man's soul into God. Their right and wrong were in Him. If they ate of the tree it would cause their soul to become dysfunctional by becoming its own agent. It would ultimately separate them from God.

When they ate of the tree their soul became isolated and anchored to the flesh. Now that they were unanchored they would now be tossed to and fro like the waves of the ocean (Eph 4:14) which causes them to be unstable in all their ways (James 1:6-8). The soul became the master and its only desire is to please itself at all cost. The unanchored soul has a hard time trusting others and God.

Certain scripture came to me about how Jesus is our "hope of Glory" (Col 1:27) and that hope is the "anchor of our soul" (Heb 6:19). Jesus became our hope to anchor us back into the Father. During His time on earth He did not please Himself but only did the will of the Father; he did not let His soul rule by bringing it under submission to His Spirit. On the cross, the tree, Jesus became the anchor nailing our soul, the flesh, back into the Father so we would no longer be tossed around. Once again the tree secured the soul of man into God.

I heard a minister say once, "The soul makes a terrible master but a great servant." The soul's function was to serve the spirit of man and the tree of knowledge kept it anchored in service. This is why Jesus came as a servant in order to gain mastery over the soul to bring it back into submission to the spirit breaking it free from the isolation of self.

The unanchored soul moves in self-sufficiency according to its own understanding; lacking trust. Proverbs three tells us to lean on and trust in God, and not rely on our own insight and understanding. But we need to know and recognize Him in all our ways and He will direct our path. It will be His direction not ours. It actually brings health to us when we do not lean on our own understanding. Things can't get clearer than that. I shiver to think how much of my life has been lived according to my understanding.

Excitement filled the room as the Aglow Area Team discussed the night's meeting with our speaker. The retreat's theme that year was about how each woman was the fragrance of God. Our hope was to bring each person into a deeper understanding of her importance to God. Weeks prior I felt Holy Spirit wanted us to anoint everyone with oil and release God's fragrance within. As a worshiper my heart naturally gravitated toward doing the anointing during worship and we planned accordingly.

As we sat around talking, my dear friend and team member said, "Sheila I think we should do the anointing after our speaker shares."

My stomach drew up into a knot as I countered back, "Well, the anointing flows better in the context of worship. Everyone is already engaged in the Spirit of God". All I could think was that anointing after the speaker wasn't what I had originally envisioned.

"You know, Sheila, I agree it should be after the speaker," stated another team member which was followed by the others agreeing with a "yes."

Frustration was brimming inside me as I encountered their words.

"But you do what you feel is best, I think it should be after," came the final words before we left our room to begin the meeting. As worship progressed I could feel the tug of war within me as thoughts raced over what had been said and how I had envisioned it to be. Then Holy Spirit spoke clearly to me and said, "Unity is more important than you doing what you think is right." The piercing words brought my frustration to an immediate halt. My team was going to let me do it when I wanted, but it was more important for me to trust my team and let go of my limited understanding. It wasn't about what I thought; it was about what our team thought. It was trusting that my team heard from God also. God has called us into unity with one another not as lone rangers isolated in our own wisdom. At that point I knew the anointing was to happen after the speaker so I submitted. The anointing time became a powerful moment and its purpose was realized.

Would it have been as powerful during worship? Maybe. But I would have missed the significant lesson of yielding my ways to God and trusting His ability to speak through other people. God showed up in a greater measure when I yielded my will and we acted as a team in unity. That is the greater purpose…to trust one another.

Distrust keeps all of us disconnected even though Jesus dealt with it on the cross. Jesus' prayer in John 17 was that we would all become one. In other words He wants the isolation and distrust among us to cease. When we lack trust of one another, it separates us into our own world of judgment towards one another, isolated in our own self-sufficiency. If God doesn't mind interacting with those we don't agree with then why do we have a problem? Maybe it's because He isn't afraid of their differing opinions. He knows He has already reconciled all men back to Himself, and He is actively drawing everyone into that understanding. He sees everyone already completed in Him.

Learning to trust God and others sends us on a journey lower taking us to where we are lifted up in Christ.

The Cover-up

The slanted words of the serpent lured Adam and Eve away from God's truth into the assumption that something was missing within them. The self-evident choice to correct the fabricated problem was to gain wisdom from the tree of knowledge. Surely that would take care of anything missing from their life.

Immediately after eating from the tree of knowledge they realized there was really nothing missing. But because they had acted upon their own knowledge and not God's, something did go missing. This was foreign to them. It felt awkward. Perplexed, they sought to cover their newly formed insecurity and inferiority - insecure in their connection with God and inferior in who they were.

Needing to hide their new state of nakedness they grabbed fig leaves as their solution. When they heard God approaching for their customary walk, the fig leaves suddenly felt insufficient. Fear reverberated within them that God would discover their altered disobedient state. So the trees became their obvious last minute hiding option. But, God was not caught unaware for He already knew what had transpired.

Likewise, most of us are actually familiar with the use of fig leaves even though we might not call it such. Unknowingly we often attempt to cover up our own insecurity and inferiority. We live in fear of exposure; isolated behind our fig leaves of self-effort.

Self-preservation is the moving force fueling the need to apply fig leaves. Adam and Eve sought to protect themselves by blaming someone else. Adam blamed God and the woman. Eve blamed the serpent even though she correctly named the true perpetrator, she still did not own up to her own wrong. It became the blame game where it had to be the fault of someone other than themselves. Life today and throughout history overflows with the blame game in action to preserve self. It's also the fig leaves of today.

Jim was good at his job but he often displayed a cocky overconfidence in himself. This particular day's work load was crazy busy with the demands of a deadline pressuring everyone in the office. Like all other days the completed paperwork was routed through the senior analyst, Frank, to double check for accuracy. As Frank previewed Jim's work he discovered an error in the figures. Lunch was fast approaching so Frank moved quickly to catch Jim before he left. The deadline was that day at 5:00 pm so there was no time to wait. It had to be done now. He found Jim shoving papers into a file as he was grabbing his coat. Hurriedly he said, "Jim, I have a question about your numbers."

"Those numbers are correct. I triple checked them". Jim countered.

"I'm sorry but I found a discrepancy in the totals of columns A and C on line fifteen," Frank said. "They don't agree."

"Frank, I don't have time for this. I have to meet someone for lunch and I have a stack of folders to finish by 5:00 this afternoon," combativeness seeped from Jim's words. "I did not make a mistake. I'm done with it," he flatly stated.

Irritation was beginning to build in Frank, "I'm sorry, but I feel it is wrong. Check it again. Look at the original figures on the client's information. Maybe you entered the wrong figure."

"You know I have a good memory. I entered the right numbers!" The nagging fear someone would accuse him of failure crept in. It triggered recollections of the many years his father constantly pointed out his imperfection by pushing him to never make a mistake. The awakened memories ignited anger that was apparent in Jim's voice, "There is no need for you to be concerned. I've got to go!"

"Go to lunch, but give me the original numbers from the client. I will look it over while you are gone," Frank sternly stated as he unrelentingly stared into his eyes. Jim's eyes faltered, he reluctantly grabbed the client's stack of folders and shoved them into Frank's outstretched hand. "I entered the correct numbers. You'll see," Jim said as he ducked out the door. The thought that anyone would think he made a mistake tore at him.

As Frank looked over the figures he found the numbers had indeed been interchanged and were incorrect. Jim didn't make very many mistakes but when he did he had a hard time admitting it. Frank wasn't looking forward to the exchange he knew was coming.

Too often people who appear to be confident are really insecure. It is self preservation at all cost, even to the detriment of others. They have to overcompensate for what they feel is missing in their lives by adding a prideful layer of fig leaves. They most often fear people will discover any inadequacies lurking below the cover-up. At times they blame someone or something instead of acknowledging the shortcoming.

Fig leaves come in many different variations: such as self-pity, addictions and even humor. Self-pity in a person will keep the focus on themselves; either they will demand constant attention on their problem or they will appear to be humble. Some people fear letting others see their true heart because they don't want to be hurt again so they might display anger keeping them away. Sometimes addictions cover up self-hatred when there is a very low opinion of themselves. Then at times some people will use excessive joking to hide the emptiness within. The list is limitless. We all have some measure of insecurity and inferiority hiding beneath tightly tucked fig leaves.

Exposure isn't very popular. All of mankind has in one degree or another participated in covering up something in their lifetime. In the Old Testament we find that King David carried out one of the biggest cover-ups known to man.

Sleep was escaping King David. Feeling restless he got up from his bed. He couldn't keep from thinking about his men on the battlefield. The reports he was receiving were very favorable. Circumstances had required him to stay in Jerusalem and it felt strange not being with them.

He was beginning to feel hemmed in by the walls of the house. The need for fresh air began to overtake him…the air might clear his thoughts. The cool wind hit his face as he broke through the door to the roof of his house. The smell of the outdoor air brought back memories of the countless nights he had slept under the stars. Often the roof was his retreat when he wanted to be alone. He gazed across Jerusalem with its white buildings resting under the star lit sky. The city stood silent with only a few scattered lights shining in the windows.

The light from a house close by grabbed his attention. Peering closer through the window he could see a woman bathing. Her stunning beauty made him tremble with excitement. He couldn't take his eyes from her as the impulses of his body screamed to feel her soft skin next to his; he wanted her. Who was she? What was her name? He had to meet her.

The events from that night set into motion the cover-up of all cover-ups. Using his power King David soon had identified the woman as Bathsheba. In a short time he had what he wanted…Bathsheba in his chamber quieting the roar of his desire. He could hide her sharing his bed until she became pregnant with his child. Her husband was one of his leaders and had been out in battle for months so it became impossible to hide. His first fig leaf cover-up fell apart as Bathsheba's husband, Uriah, refused to take comfort in his wife's arms because his men slept on the ground far away. Everyone would know the child was not her husband's. He couldn't let anyone know.

This led to an even greater fig leaf cover-up…murder. He arranged for Uriah to die on the battlefield; hoping it would look like a unfortunate incident. He applied another layer of fig leaves.

King David was bent on hiding his atrocities from others. The guilt was relentless, driving him to hide the more, but the fig leaf was destined to come off. It began to roll back as the prophet Nathan began exposing the cover-up. In the midst of King David's exposure he cried out in repentance. In the midst of his anguish, God's loving forgiveness covered his wrong. When he gave up doing things his way, in his own understanding, with no more cover-ups, he could then receive God's kindness toward him. (2 Sam 11:1-12: 13).

Even after King David's ultimate cover-up, God still chose to use Bathsheba and David as the lineage of Jesus.

How could this be? Why would God do that? It was David's heart. When David allowed the fig leaves removal and owned up to his wrong then God could pour through him the lineage of His Son. No cover-up by man; no fig leaves.

This account was God's way of telling us that He has the answer to our fig leaf dilemma; He has His own covering for our wrongs…the blood of Jesus. It is a healing balm undoing all the wrongs of mankind. He says, "Bring it on! Give Me your fig leaves. I have the solution for any and every cover-up but first you must quit hiding and come to Me". There is no cover-up He cannot deal with. We just have to be willing to let go. The way to go lower is to stop playing the cover-up game.

3 The Aftermath

Splinter or Log?

In Matthew 7, Jesus said not to judge one another. He talked about how we should not look at the splinter in our brother's eye when we have a log in our own. He said, first, we are to take the log out of our eye so we can see clearly to help take the splinter out of our brother's eye. This scripture was magnified to me through an experience that brought greater understanding to its meaning.

The day was unusually warm for the Oregon coast in October. My feet sloshed through the foamy waves sending a tingling numbness through my feet - making the frigid water, surprisingly bearable. I loved how the sand ebbed away from under my toes as the water was swept back into the ocean. I had been walking for miles in dialogue with Holy Spirit.

Hurt and betrayal ached in my heart. My husband and I had entrusted a couple with leadership in our ministry. After the sting of past relationships it had been refreshing to have someone beside us again. But they in time began to accuse us and became critical. Hurt by relationship again.

As I poured out my confused hurt to God, He quietly began to reveal a truth that changed my response to people and situations from that point on. I was surprised to learn my hurt did not come from them but from the wounds in my own heart.

To bring greater clarification to this thought, there is a basic principle which explains why we react the way we do to certain things in life. If you lay two acoustic guitars near each other and you pluck the 'A' string on one guitar then the 'A' string on the second guitar will begin to vibrate of its own accord. The 'A' strings share the same frequency so they naturally respond to one another.

Likewise, the wounds in our heart pick up the wounded frequency of others. The natural response is to blame our reaction on them when we get angry, hurt or belittled. It is easy to say, they made me angry; they hurt my feelings; they made me feel incompetent. But in reality it is the insecurity and inferiority of our own heart vibrating on the same frequency of others' insecurity and inferiority. These wounds keep us focused on self. Then fig leaves are produced to hide and protect our injured soul. Fig leaves are good deflectors. It puts the situation onto the other person by believing it's their fault. Often, we don't even know we are doing it.

But, what if we allowed God to heal the wounds of our heart? If our wounds were healed and absent then people could say or do anything and we would not respond because that frequency of hurt would no longer live in our heart. There would be no need to divert attention from our hurts by blaming others. We would not be affected by it and would respond differently in those difficult times.

I found that when I am hurt or angry with someone or something it is an opportunity for God to reveal the hidden wounds in me so He can heal them. I began to ask myself, "Okay, why did you respond that way? Why did you feel pain, rejection or anger? Holy Spirit will you please reveal any wounds in need of healing?" The result was amazing. To me this has been much more effective than any long detailed inner healing program available. I must say that these programs have helped people but we are moving into a time when we need to learn how to govern our own soul and take authority over it. We end up relying on others and a program to do the job for us. It is time for the body of Christ to grow up into the fullness of Christ Jesus.

This is what Jesus was talking about when He said, "The enemy has nothing in me." (John 14:30). There were no soul wounds or self-focus the enemy could tap into; no injured frequency within Him. In one of my favorite shows the main character needs to obtain information quickly from the villain he apprehended. He applies pressure to an existing or new wound using the pain to force them to tell what they know. As they scream out in pain from the interrogation they give him the information he wants. Similarly, when there are wounds in our heart Satan applies pressure to our injuries which causes our soul to scream in pain. Most of the time we don't realize our wounds cause us to respond the way we do. But, what if the wounds were completely healed? With no wounds Satan would have nothing to apply pressure to; having nothing in us. Being healed we would not respond to others injured soul. We would be on a different frequency.

I began to ask Holy Spirit to reveal to me the wounds in my own heart that caused me respond the way I did. As He began to reveal instances in my past I invited Him to move over the wounded areas and bring healing. The effectiveness of this surprised me greatly. I began to notice my responses when I was angry, hurt, or felt inadequate and then I would allow Holy Spirit to heal my injuries. After a few years of walking in this practice I can honestly say people can and have said hurtful things to me but I respond differently than I used to. The wounds are fewer so there is less for Satan to apply pressure to. There is becoming more and more of "nothing in me" that he can access. Have I arrived? No…but I'm closer than I was.

On the beach that day God highlighted still another truth. God pointed out pride at work in my wounded response. As I explored this thought I could clearly see I feared that these people did not like me because of their view of me. Their opinion was much too important so it gave birth to pride through my self-focus and wounds. I wanted them to think well of me. So when they came against me, pride rose up to defend my own wounded heart. Pride can only be defeated by giving up self-will and self-focus allowing our heart to be healed. Again, I allowed

Holy Spirit to come in and begin to remove the pride within me.

Often our first response is to focus on what the other person is doing or not doing. It's so easy to find fault in others before we see our own imperfection. This parable says the other person's splinter is small because it isn't yours to deal with; it's up to God. It doesn't mean they are without fault, but their splinter is for God to deal with…in His way. God calls us to take care of what is going on in our heart, not someone else's. Too often we don't realize the real perpetrator is our own log of wounds. By focusing on their splinter the issue shifts off of us becoming a fig leaf to hide our wounds.

Actually, if we are willing, difficult situations can become a tool of God's refining and healing. It is a situation where God can turn what the enemy intended for evil into good. (Gen 15:20). We would do well by turning to Holy Spirit so He can guide us into wholeness. Letting God deal with the log in our lives is the path to lower so we can be lifted into God's higher.

The Blame Game

The blame game. It's a game mankind has played from the beginning of time. Every human is invited to play in one way or another. Sometimes it is very apparent and at other times it goes unnoticed, much like a second nature. What is the blame game really all about? It began with a certain snake in a garden where he introduced a lie through an opposing thought. But it was Adam and Eve, in the midst of their God-like splendor, who listened and decided to play the lies game. To understand what the blame game is we need to look at its inception in the garden.

As the fruit lay shimmering in his hand Adam knew it would be sweet and juicy. His mouth began watering at the thought. He had passed by this tree many times eying its luscious fruit. Curiosity enlivened his thoughts as to what such divine fruit would taste like. The words of the serpent were still ringing in his mind, "surely you will not die; you will be like God knowing good and evil."

Eve had just eaten the fruit. She then handed it to him whispering, "We were told it will make us wise. There must be more wisdom than what God has told us about.

See, I ate and nothing is different. We will be able to tend the earth in a better capacity."

Looking at her he said, "You're not dying like God said. Maybe there are things God is holding back from us? So maybe we will be wiser..." Adam's stunned look was apparent as he stared at the fruit in his hand. Seeing no change in Eve left him feeling numb with the unexpected outcome.

Echoing in his mind were God's instructions, not to eat of the tree of knowledge. But, nothing happened to Eve. Looking into her smiling face he remembered his ecstatic delight when he first laid eyes on her. She was more than he could imagine. The penetrating beauty of her eyes seemed to reach down into his very soul awakening a part of him as only she could. God had taken her from his own body, building her to perfection; she was his protector and nurturer. He had found himself in her as they embraced one another's uniqueness. God had specifically forbidden him to eat the fruit, but the woman, whom God had given him, said they would be wiser. After all, she was his protection; why shouldn't he trust her?

He closed his eyes as the debate resounded in his mind. He could sense the life of every living creature and plant swirling in unison within him. The pulsating light of God's glory, intertwined with his spirit, blanketing his outer body. Within himself there was an awareness of the activity of all life on earth and in heaven; he could hear it...feel it...this was all he had ever known.

The debate was over as he sank his teeth into the fruit sending its juices running across his lips, exploding the flavor within his mouth. The sweetness was self-gratifying as he chewed. What's that? Silence. Everything in and around him seemed to come to a screeching halt. The familiar voice of the earth became deafeningly quiet. He felt separated, isolated, and alone as he frantically looked around. Looking at his hands he could see something different about his body, it didn't vibrate with light, his muscle laid bare. The light of his spirit was gone. The body's covering was removed. The continual presence of God had left...he felt naked...exposed.

Looking at woman he could see she had experienced the same disconnect as he had, the same silence. Her appearance had changed; she looked different. Like his, her sinew and muscle was now exposed. Where was the vibrant light that surrounded her? Why had he trusted her? This is her fault and God's fault because He gave her to me as my companion. (I go into more detail about the exposed sinew in the chapter entitled, "Restoration").

A loud groan escaped from their lips as they fell in a heap flinging their hands over their heads. Realization stung as they cried, "We should have listened to God!" The awareness of their actions shook the core of their being. Guilt and shame flooded them as they attempted to hide their naked bodies with their squirming arms and hands. Quickly they began grabbing leaves to fasten them to their body in whatever way they could. In desperation they were compelled to hide their changed appearance. They didn't want God to know they had not listened to Him.

Then they heard the sound of God coming, in His customary way, to walk in the garden with them. Suddenly the leaves seemed insufficient. Quickly they took refuge among the bushes hiding themselves among its thickness.

"Adam where are you?" God called out. (As if God didn't already know).

Hesitantly from behind the trees Adam answered, "I heard your sound and I was afraid because I was naked so I hid myself."

"Who told you that you were naked? Did you eat of the tree I told you not to eat of?" God obviously knew the answer as He asked the question.

Resentment rose up within Adam as he said, "It was the woman you prepared to be at my side; she gave me the fruit and I ate it." Anger began to grow as his thoughts raced, *After all, God shouldn't have given him someone that would mislead him.*

God said to the woman, "What have you done?"

"The serpent deceived me," her voice wavered as the heaviness of her choice weighed upon her. She hung her head in guilt. (Gen 3).

The original state of Adam and Eve had changed; they were not the same as before. The earth followed suit in the transposition. With this came the blame game in full swing. Each one was flinging blame by pointing out the others imperfection. Adam put the blame on the woman and

God. Eve put it onto the serpent. No one wanted to own up to their own mistake. Diligently they hid their own lack by focusing on the other person's flaw. The fig leaf of blame was used to hide their shortcoming.

Just as Adam and Eve played the blame game we too, at times, play the same game; blaming others for our situation or problem. I have talked with some people, who received secular counseling, who were told that their parents were at fault for how they turned out. Also, I have heard how others were told that the harsh surroundings in which they grew up were to blame for their outcome. Fig leaves are used to cover the insecurity and inferiority by blaming others.

There are some people who get mad and blame their anger on the actions of others by claiming they made them mad. They won't own up to the guilt of their own anger. Then there are times some will accuse others or the circumstances to divert it from themselves. It becomes another fig leaf to hide the true condition of their heart. Yes, one's upbringing does feed into people's tendencies but anyone can make the choice to not respond to what has been handed to them. Let God heal your heart so you can be free to make good choices. By removing the fig leaf and facing change, we can leave the old patterns behind.

At times shifting the blame can be seen at work in abusive situations. Some abused wives will excuse their husband's actions by laying the blame on themselves or the circumstance even though they could be in danger. Too often she refuses to acknowledge the problem and even pretends it doesn't exist. This is her makeshift fig leaf to hide the hurt and pain from herself and others.

Also, the abuse of drugs can cause users to blame others for why they do what they do. The addiction gives any excuse to feed itself. Shifting the blame keeps users in bondage to the problem. It is easy to hide behind the fig leaf of blame to cover shame and failure.

The blame game shows up in subtle ways. For instance, in my life, it has presented itself when I have attempted to explain why I arrived late to an event. I must admit, I tend to get lost in getting ready and not noticing the time. As the years have gone by thankfully I have improved. One main thing that helped me change was when I realized the reason I don't like to arrive early is because I might have to wait. So, then I leave too late. Most of the time, it was easy to throw a fig leaf over the real reason by placing blame on a phone call, too much to get done, traffic was bad, I couldn't decide what to wear and the list goes on. There is always something to dump the blame onto. Unconsciously, excuses spilled out of my mouth in an attempt to shift the fault from me. After all it is easier to blame someone or something other than myself. Bottom line is that I made wrong choices. I could have decided to keep an eye on the time or get over my not liking to arrive early. The use of fig leaves comes naturally to most of us in very subtle ways.

Mankind's fleshly inclination, too often, is to hide their faults among one's self-centeredness. Unknowingly, it is easy to act as the "all sufficient one" absorbed by our own wisdom and perception. Wasn't it the search to be wise that led to the blame game cover-up in the first place? At times we scurry to hide our faults and weaknesses in any way we can so we apply the fig leaf.

This search for significance, through our own wisdom, actually keeps us separated from who we were created to be. This self-absorption causes our true identity to remain elusive; separated by a fig leaf to lift ourselves above others. Lurking deep within mankind is the hidden belief that we don't measure up. Through the blame game our tendency is to produce fig leaves to hide our deficiency from ourselves and others. Within us the memory of how we were significantly made in His likeness still exists, but hidden. So we lift ourselves up into a self-induced significance instead of going lower by laying down our self-focus. Our very being still carries the knowledge of our need for His completeness...His oneness...His significance.

Jesus nailed our selfish tendencies on the cross where we died with Him. He shifted our blame onto Himself as He said, "Father, forgive them for they know not what they do." How often do we have that response? The blame game ended as He overcame the self-will of man. He removed our fig leaves by removing what they hid and covered us with His blood...His purity. With this action He gave us the freedom to come face to face with the Father; nothing separating us. We can now walk in the cool of the day, once again, with God in the garden of His heart.

Unwittingly, we at times bring to life what Jesus already put to death by joining the accuser in the blame game. So, next time when blame is unholstered will we say, "Father forgive them they do not know what they are doing" or will we fling blame instead? Let's quit playing that game by throwing off the fig leaves of blame and begin to once again experience the completeness and oneness with the Father and all of creation.

The way up is by laying down that age old blame game tendency.

Hood of Suspicion

Just as Adam and Eve chose to be wise in themselves we likewise navigate life through our own wisdom. If most people think they are the only ones that hold all the answers then no wonder we can't get along because everyone thinks he or she is right. This action devalues others and exalts ourselves. There is the perception within us humans that our understanding is unmistakably precise. This perception pulls the hood of suspicion over our head blinding us.

We all have a limited perception. There is a video where two groups are in a circle. One group is wearing white and the other is dressed in black. Each group is passing a basketball back and forth to one another within their group. The audience is asked to count how many times the balls are tossed by the group dressed in white. After the groups stop tossing the ball the audience is asked if they saw the gorilla that walked through the middle of the circle. Most people do not see the gorilla because their focus is on the balls. This is an undeniable example showing the limitation of what we notice when our focus is on a certain thing. How often has our dogmatic view been a result of our biased focus? What could we be missing because we think our perception is correct? I guarantee we are all missing a tremendous amount of things in every situation. This is why we need God's wisdom and not our own. Also, this is why we desperately need each other.

Throughout my many years of marriage my husband and I have disagreed on whether a particular color was blue or green. We both have been unswervingly adamant about how we interpreted the color. Why were we convinced our view was the correct view? We were isolated in our own wisdom believing our perception was correct. Science tells us that each individual can see colors differently. It is how our bodies function. So who is right? It's all subject to our personal makeup.

Sandra stood at the lookout gazing at the city where she and her husband, Rick, were called to. Excited anticipation bubbled up inside her being. She had already had many dreams in the night from God about what He wanted to do. Warmth filled her as she could feel Rick's presence beside her. She had been alone for a number of years which made her feel even more appreciative of the man God had miraculously given her. Now there was someone to share this new journey with.

They settled into the life of the community, gathering many who shared the same vision to usher in a move of God. They were hopeful to come into relationship with seemingly like minded pastors.

Like many other events, they scheduled a night of worship, renting a meeting room. This particular night they had invited outside speakers and the event promised to be a big night of celebration. Planning was in full swing as the date drew near.

The phone vibrated in Sandra's pocket as she was looking over the meeting's agenda. It was one of the pastors they had begun to build a relationship with. "Hello, Sam how are you doing?" Sandra asked.

"Doing good. I need to set up a time to talk with you and Rick." Sam's voice sounded strained. "It needs to be soon."

Uneasiness began to squelch her excitement, "Sure. We are free tonight. Can you come to our house tonight?"

"Tonight will work for me. How about seven o'clock?' Sam asked.

"Okay, see you at seven." Sandra whispered.

Over the past few months Sam had begun to feel uneasy about Rick and Sandra's meetings. He loved their excitement when they were around, but in his opinion they were acting independently and were not under the covering of a pastor. They needed to have the okay of their pastor before they had all these meetings. It was dangerous for them and the community to be independently doing meetings. Also, he had been receiving phone calls from other pastors who were voicing this same concern. It was an overall opinion that their church members were being asked to be involved too much in these meetings. There was a fear that the members would neglect the meetings of their own church. Something had to change.

Rick and Sandra listened to Sam's concerns as disbelief reverberated within them. The vision God had given them began to lose its breath in the tightening chokehold. Their hands were being tied behind their backs. Why would God give them a vision for this city if they had to wait for a pastor to okay their every move? Was this a call given to them or to a pastor? Were they going to continue with what God had called them to and make the pastors mad or were they going to fold under the scrutiny of another man's opinion? Was God's call higher than another man's opinion? They were at a crossroads.

The pastor was only responding from what he had been taught about the function of a leader. It is a noble concept to protectively watch over those you are leading, but this idea actually minimizes Holy Spirit from working in an individual's life, teaching them they can't hear as well as the leader. Also, this concept usually produces a fear that they might incorrectly hear what is coming to them. When Holy Spirit came into the earth He didn't enter into only a few so they could be the voice of Holy Spirit to guide others. He came to guide *all* men into the Truth, not just a select few, but *all.* (John 16:13). Everyone of us has the ability to hear Holy Spirit just as clearly as the other person. The only difference is that some may be more practiced than others at hearing.

Because we think someone else hears better than us, we tend to fade into the background waiting to be called upon; waiting to finally be able to hear as well as others. And then leaders wonder why they can't motivate people to come off the pews and participate. Could they only be responding from how they've been taught? Sit and wait.

What would it be like if leaders encouraged their people to listen and do what they feel Holy Spirit is directing them to do, even if the leader doesn't understand? I think we would be astounded at the advancement of God's kingdom. Leaders are there to show the people how to hear for themselves; to be their counsel, not their ears.

Years ago I heard a teaching by Graham Cooke where he talked about how the vision of the church is not the vision of the pastor but actually is the vision that is within its people. When each person functions in their God given destiny and what Holy Spirit is saying to them personally then that is the vision for that body of believers. The pastor is to draw out the vision of the people and release them in it. If leaders functioned from this mindset then they would not put on the hood of suspicion and constrain their people from what they are hearing for themselves.

When Holy Spirit was sent into every believer He wrote God's law upon every heart so that each individual would know and hear God. (Hebrews 8: 10,11). Then why do people insist upon hearing God for others? By someone forcing their opinions and view on others, it actually devalues who God created them to be. No one will come into their destiny apart from others. So when we limit people in who they are, we really are limiting our destiny, too.

Sadly, at times I too have been hesitant to trust those in the religious community because of their teaching. When it doesn't line up with what God has shown me, then I tend to put on a hood of suspicion. I have measured them through my own wisdom and understanding. We all hear and know in part. Not one of us has the full picture of what God is doing in each of our lives. No one man, church or ministry will be given a complete revelation from God. Each one of us represents one piece of the puzzle in which God is revealing His final design. I limit God's plan through my limited view and judgments of others. It is a hood of suspicion that isolates and keeps us from trusting one another.

Our judgments bring isolation in many ways. Simple events judged by our own wisdom will skew our perception. It has always been a challenge for me to be the passenger in a car. The movement of the driver appears too fast and in need of more control. So, I end up uncomfortably nervous. Is it because they are bad drivers or because I have my own perception about their driving? In reality, I am isolated in my limited wisdom and view. My experience becomes the measure of their success behind the wheel. I am left with a miniscule perspective of the actual occurrence. I trust more in my own reason so I miss what is truly happening; my view is misinterpreted.

"Be not wise in your own eyes" (Prov 3:7) is the prescription for reinstated trust in God and others. It is the key to restoring true trust found only in the Father. When our trust is reestablished in God then we can begin to trust one another by stepping out of our microscopic wisdom; out of our isolated-self. Why? Maybe it's because we aren't seeing the full picture.

Through the years I have found it very important to trust what others are hearing from God. Who knows what kind of mess I would be in now if I hadn't! I discuss further trusting others in the chapter, "Jesus in Others".

Taking off this hood of suspicion is the road to going lower where all are released in the importance of their destiny. The way up is down. Let's lay down our suspicion so God can lift us higher into Him and His purpose.

Approval Game

Most everyone on planet earth has played the approval game at one time or another even though we don't realize we have participated. This inherited tendency is a subtle game.

Why do people seek the approval of man or even of God? It is the search for security and significance. Adam and Eve lost their security in God when they quit trusting Him, launching them into the isolation of self-trust. When isolated we are left with our limited perception trying to create security and worth in the things we do. The need for significance leads us into promoting ourselves in the sight of others. Our need for approval becomes a fig leaf hiding insecurity deep within.

In our search for acceptance we at times push ourselves to perfection which hides the insecurity imbedded within. This need for perfection is seen in business, entertainment, politics, school, the church and actually in most arena's of life. It's the game to lift ourselves higher through self-effort. Sometimes this game becomes quite ugly and harmful.

Roxanne sat in the plush waiting room filled to the max. Inconspicuously, she perused the room from the corner of her eye taking inventory of those who were auditioning for the same role as she.

Her thoughts raced, "Psh! Nicole is here! She has always had it out for me. She is constantly pushing herself onto the directors and the producers. Her mouth won't shut up; she is always talking about herself!" Irritation was burning inside her as she shifted her tightly clad hips in the chair sending her multiple chained necklace clinking.

Nicole slowly rose to her feet as if to make a simple movement melodramatic. Her eyes locked onto Roxanne with a smirk sweeping across her face as she approached.

"Roxanne! I am so surprised to see you here," Nicole gushed as she adjusted her tight fitting jacket exposing more of her revealing neckline. "I would have thought this role was a little beyond your expertise. You've never played this type of character before. Couldn't it prove to be too big of a challenge for you?"

The tall slender figure towered over Roxanne. Holding back the anger brimming on her lips she said, "Nicole, I am very prepared for this role. You have miscalculated my experience. You're just worried I will get the part leaving you out in the dark!" Roxanne's words smoothed her fury as she crossed her long legs clad in stiletto boots. She calmly adjusted the jeweled bracelet hanging loosely on her wrist as she glared intently at Nicole.

Nicole's eyes flashed as they narrowed behind long black lashes. Roxanne thought, *It's a wonder she can see when she does that!*

As Nicole sidled away with a whispered snarl she said, "Believe me, I will get the role! I have friends. They know I'm perfect for it." A smile decorated her face as she crossed the room. Grasping her short skirt she floated back into her chair.

The familiar grinding of inadequacy rumbled in Roxanne's stomach; the fear of failure. Ever since she could remember her mom hounded her when she made a mistake. Her mother's voice reverberated in her memory, *Roxanne, what will people think? The only way to get ahead in life is to show people you are good at what you do. That is where the prestige and money are. No one wants to see weakness, so shape up. You might be rejected if you don't!*

Throughout High School the drive to participate in almost every sport and play compelled her. All she had ever known was a tight schedule of practice and performance. Each competition presented the dreaded "pep talk" from Mom whether she won or lost. Compliments from her Mom were few and far between designed to push her beyond her limits. At times Roxanne longed to relax and be a normal person. Normal? What was that? If it was staring her in the face would she even recognize it?

She glanced around at the familiar scene; a room full of people, waiting to audition. This was the only life she had ever known. The need to surpass the other person vibrated in the atmosphere. She wasn't so sure she could survive without it. It was her prod to try harder to insure her success.

Roxanne's story represents many people; some worse, some better. The need to perform lays within most everyone and is not easily recognized because it comes in every shape, size and color.

Not only is this approval game played in measurement of ourselves but also in measuring others. Do they meet "my" approval? Often when someone believes or does something different than what we do or believe then it is easy to stamp them "unapproved". If it is not up to one person's standard then we don't trust them or it is wrong.

You can find this approval game even in the simplest everyday activities. When cutting vegetables my husband just wants to get it done so they will be thick and unevenly cut. I on the other hand like thin small pieces which I believe are easier to fit onto my fork or sandwich. Believe me we've had a few discussions on this matter. Did cutting them differently affect the taste? No. I just didn't approve of "how" he cut them. Realizing I was playing the approval game I've learned to let it go. Life is smoother by not trying to make my husband do things my way and releasing him to do things how he likes to do them.

Too many churches play this game in some form or another. Yes there are those churches that can come together in partnership but often it is very limited within the community. Even if a church would like to embrace other churches they can't because the other church does not "approve" of them. So the game goes on ostracizing one another.

I have been to many community-wide church worship meetings. Honestly, if I worshipped the way I do in my own church I probably wouldn't be approved of by many in the meeting. Because of this opinion I have held back. This approval game keeps churches from true unity. Too many of these meetings are laden with man's endeavor to appear unified, but gets lost in the attempt to produce unity merely for unity's sake. In other words, people often are not allowed to be who they really are for fear of rejection. How is that unity? Let's face it; too often the trust factor is super low between churches. The measurement or approval of others negates the unity Jesus prayed for in John 17. We, at times, do not trust in others ability to hear from God or that God could actually be for them.

In the approval game often people will not trust those who have a different doctrinal view. I have witnessed this time after time in my decades of church life. There are even times people actually leave churches because something was said which they did not agree with. On comes the hood of suspicion. It's different from how I believe, so it must be wrong. Or even the times someone was cut off from a group because they believed a slightly different thought than everyone else.

Sadly, I too also have kept people at arm's length when their doctrine was different than mine. But, one thing I've noticed is that God does not remove Himself from working in people who hold a different scriptural doctrine than mine. Or, God forbid, He is still with people even when they are in error. God gave me a good example of how he sees His people.

The wind raked through my hair from the open car window on the hot summer day. The sound of little girls laughing could be heard as I drove by a house. Their fun filled sound drew me to glance at where it was coming from. Two little girls about six or seven were at play on the porch. My grandmother's heart leapt with tenderness as I thought, *Oh, the sweet babies are having so much fun playing house as if they were adults.* My eyes filled with tears at the thought of how precious children were. Suddenly, I heard God say, "That is exactly how I see my children; each one at play trying to figure out how church should really be; my children pretending to be adults. I take much joy in watching them play because I know they are heading towards maturity in Me. I love all my children."

The already brimming tears began to overflow their boundary down my cheeks. Love and compassion for the body of Christ welled up within me. It was comforting to know that God isn't put off by our differences in doctrine. We all only "know in part". Not one person or church sees the big picture or has all knowledge. God chooses to use all of us to bring His kingdom to the earth; reconciling it back to Him. God has approved all of us through His Son, Jesus Christ.

The main reason we are compelled to approve or disapprove of people is really because we are in search of approval for ourselves. Somehow, we think there is a lack within us so we attempt to fill the void by tearing others down and elevating ourselves. Unknowingly, we tend to devalue people because of the lack of value we see in ourselves. At times the approval game becomes a fig leaf to hide the inferiority within us. But again, Jesus gave all of us value through His death on the cross.

Recently I was reminded of a vision I had of a net covering the whole earth. As I looked, the panoramic view zoomed in close enough so I could see that the net was made up of billions of people connected to one another by linking hands. No one person could complete this net. It took everyone. This is the unity of a bride "who has made herself ready" for the coming of her Bridegroom, Jesus. (Rev 19:7). If even one person is missing from their link in the net it leaves the net vulnerable and weak. We all have our place in this world…our own role…our own destiny.

If God has approved us then why look to man for approval? Or, yet why do we think we have to approve others? It is our search for security that leads us away from the security Jesus gave us through His shed blood. Our trust in Him gives us security. Our security was gained through what Jesus did, not by what we or others do.

When we begin to live trusting God, then we will not be looking for security in man. Trusting the Jesus in one another will cause the approval game to cease. It is the way to God through going lower.

Down the Up Staircase

4 Restoration

Truth Sets Free

Truth. From the beginning of time mankind has been in search of it. It is sought after in relationship, government, the church, business…well…actually in most areas of life. It's right there at the top of the list. At times it takes a judge and jury to somewhat find the truth. But, no matter what, truth is sought after.

Even though lying comes easy for some, no one really likes to be lied to, even those who lie. The real reason people craft lies is to hide truth. When was the first lie introduced? What was its purpose? Lies originated with the father of lies, Satan, the age old serpent, for the sole purpose to hide truth from Adam and Eve; the truth of their God DNA. Satan actually wanted what they had. It was his only chance to acquire the power he didn't have.

This is why he deceived man into believing they could find truth apart from God. Man searching for truth apart from God led them to hand over their authority to Satan; their God-given identity as governors of the earth.

If we are separated from *the* God of Truth then how can we ever really find truth apart from Him? Can we find truth in our own wisdom? No. Truth can only come from God. Adam and Eve gave entrance to mankind's separation from Truth. God passionately disliked the separation so He devised a plan even before Adam and Eve made their choice. It was a way to restore mankind back into relationship with him…to remove the lie. God's plan was Jesus.

The sneering voice weaved its way into the exhausted stupor of Jesus, "*If* You are God's Son, command these stones to be made bread." As the words aroused Him He could feel the growling rumble in His stomach. It had now been forty days since He had eaten. *Bread would taste so good right now,* He thought. Not only was He weak from hunger but the nagging repetitive words from the devil tore at Him like the incessant tree branch scratching the side of a house. All He wanted was for the taunting words to stop.

No, He couldn't listen to the lies that were being spoken. His soul wanted to lash out at the intrusion. The accuser's voice resembled the hiss of a serpent. It was Adam and Eve who first listened to the serpent's lie…not remaining in God's truth. That lie had to be rejected to break its agreement with man. He had to resist the urge to respond to the needs of His flesh. The intense pain in His heart was still pounding from Adam and Eve choosing their way instead of listening to the Father. That separation tore at His heart. Oh how He, Father, and Holy Spirit had enjoyed being with them; in a certain way man completed Them. There was much joy when They were together. The yearning love for His people pushed Him to repeat His Father's words to Himself. If He could only keep God's words in His thoughts so it would drown the lies. As the words raced within they began to spill out of His mouth, "It has been written, Man shall not live by bread alone, but by every word that comes forth from the mouth of God."

The weakness and hunger of His flesh maneuvered His soul onto the rolling waves of emotions; whether to agree with the offer or not? Maybe He should just give in just to end the turmoil. He could feel His soul teetering back and forth, assembling confusion in His mind. *No! He had to quit riding this wave of emotions!* Whispering to Himself, "I must force Myself to focus on the reason I am here; to overcome the self-willed actions of the flesh bringing truth back to mankind and to restore them to the Father."

Suddenly, Jesus' body was snatched upward out of the place He had been laying. In an instant His feet landed abruptly on top of the temple's pinnacle. A cool breeze rushed through His sweat soaked clothes sending a shiver through Him. As He gazed down at the courtyard He found it hard to stand upright from weakness. He could feel Satan nudging close to Him. A foul smell drifted into His nostrils causing Him to lean away. But, Satan pressed his face even closer as he peered into Jesus' face whispering, " *If* You are the Son of God, throw Yourself down; for it is written, He will give His angels charge over you, and they will bear you up on their hands, lest you strike your foot against a stone."

Jesus' thoughts raced, *Who does he think he is? He questions my Sonship?* Irritation reverberated in His soul as He thought, *I could really dispel this lie by showing him who I really am.* He lifted His head and closed His eyes. There He saw a picture of the throne room filled with angels as they sang praises to the Father. In the midst was His Father's throne pulsating with lights of all colors. There was a never-ending joy filling the atmosphere. He took a deep breath as if drinking in the rich memory. The thoughts made Him long for what was His before clothing Himself with this body of fallen man. It could all be His again right now, but then, mankind would be lost forever. Shaking His head in an attempt to clear His foggy thinking He began to repeat His Father's words again. He weakly lifted His quivering fingers to rub His aching forehead. *What does the Father say?* The Father's words began to flow rapidly through His mind as they gave strength to weariness. Facing the Devil He firmly stated, "On the other hand, it is written also, 'You shall not tempt the Lord your God'." He stared unwaveringly into the tempter's snarling eyes.

Again, Jesus was swiftly plucked up and deposited on a high mountain. Even in its fallen state the landscape was breathtakingly beautiful. He remembered the time He, Holy Spirit and Father created it; it was alive with color and motion. They had given dominion of it to Adam and Eve, but because of the lie they handed it over to Satan.

As the devil spread his arms wide across the view he said, "These things, all taken together, I will give you, if You will prostrate Yourself before me and do homage and worship me." A cunning smile broke across his face as he searched for Jesus' reaction.

Jesus thought, *Truly he had the right to give it because he stole it from Adam and Eve. Maybe, this could be a way He could win back the earth from this wicked clutch of Satan? But how would it win back mankind?* His soul was rising up and down in a turmoil of emotions. It made His head swim, leaving Him lightheaded. Exhaustion and hunger fed into the constant surge of emotions He was feeling. It wouldn't take much just to bow down and worship him, it would be over!

He was amazed at how easy it was to consider giving in. No, He couldn't move down this slippery slope just to satisfy His soul. Slicing through the path of His thoughts He forced Himself to think, *God's words, only God's words will cause Me to overcome the chaos of My soul. I must only rehearse what My Father says! I choose to govern my thoughts and emotions bringing them under subjection to My Spirit.* An explosion of words erupted from the depths of His being as He cried out, "Ahhh! Begone Satan! For it is written, you shall worship the Lord your God and Him alone shall you serve." The atmosphere shook with the intensity of His words. His searing glare accented His words as He leaned in close to Satan's face. Sweat poured down into His eyes stinging them, but He refused to lower His gaze.

Satan screeched in rage as he jumped back from Jesus. Glaring at Jesus he hissed, "I will find another time to get you! It's not over yet! There will still be plenty of opportunity ahead." As he fled he thought, "I have to get Him to function out of His self-will and not His spirit."

Jesus' body crumpled to the ground in complete exhaustion. As He lay lifeless the familiar hands of the Angels began to comfort and cradle Him. Their very touch began to revive His body while they gave Him nourishment from heaven. The purpose of His coming to earth began stirring once again within Him, to reconcile man back to God, the ones They love more than life itself. (Matt 4:1-11; Lk 4: 1-13).

It is interesting that Satan attacked Jesus' identity in the same way he attacked Adam and Eve's. He was gambling that Jesus would trade his identity by seeking truth within Himself instead of functioning from God's Truth. After all, the plan was very successful before why not again? But, Satan lost that wager when Jesus trumped the lie by remaining in the Father's truth.

Jesus restored Truth to the fallen world. He came to reconcile man back to his original position in God (2 Cor 5: 18). Jesus Christ, the Truth (John 14:6), completely set us free (John 8:32) from the lie through His death and resurrection. He has fully restored us back into our rightful position in God, the Father. It is Jesus, the Truth, that reversed the lie.

We were created in God's very own image; a triune being, *spirit, soul* and *body* put on earth to govern. But, we were separated from the truth of this identity when Adam and Eve handed their God DNA to Satan. That stolen identity empowered him to rule over all that pertained to the earth. Our spirit was stripped from its reign over the soul leaving us vulnerable to the meager existence of life according to the flesh; subservient to an *inferior life* instead of a *superior life* as ruling spirit beings. We were left groveling over the search for truth within our own wisdom; a self-focused life; separated from our purpose. Today, Satan's lie still tricks us into leaving God's truth.

But, the Truth, Jesus Christ, re-established us back into our true God DNA setting us free from the rule of our flesh. (Romans 8:5,13-14). When we embrace our identity, then and only then, can we function in authority over this earth as Sons of the living God. It is up to God's Sons to reconcile the world back to the Father covering the earth with His Truth.

Then why do we still struggle if Jesus has conquered the flesh? It's because Satan still unceasingly continues to weave his lies into the very fabric of our life which attempts to hide God's truth. Truly, it is merely a lie that keeps us from the freedom that we already own. We just haven't apprehended it yet. Believing a paltry lie keeps the truth hidden so we will continue to hand over our God DNA to empower Satan; without it he is powerless. Without our agreement the devil can do nothing. The lies will be silenced when we lay hold of Jesus, the Truth, and then we can live according to the Spirit where victory is a sure reality.

Jesus overcame Satan's lie by lowering Himself and there He founded man back into God's Truth.

Trust Restored

When truth was reestablished through Christ Jesus,

trust could once again function. Trust naturally follows truth because truth is trustworthy. (Psalm 91:4). If one is not living in God's truth then distrust will hold sway over that person's life. When Adam and Eve refused to listen to God's truth then trust was lost. Trust went out the door with truth. From that point on so went the generations of mankind; finding it hard to trust anyone but self.

The raging wind lashed through the water generating waves that towered above the lone boat in the dark night. The small vessel rolled and rocked with the pounding of each wave. The men gripped the boat's edge working frantically to stay afloat and not wash overboard.

Where was Jesus? Peter thought. *He said He would join us shortly after insisting we go back across the sea. I would feel so much safer if He was here.*

The sky had long grown dark with the night, but the storm made it even blacker than usual. Fear could be seen as Jesus' disciples frantically secured the now rolled up sails. The violent storm had pounced upon them leaving them scrambling to survive. Any speech was muted in the raging wind leaving them to communicate with hand signals. It was good that many of the men were seasoned fisherman who knew what to do under the circumstances.

Each one kept a close watch on the dark water surrounding them. One never knew when they could be driven into another vessel. Suddenly one of the men yelled, "What's that? It looks like a man! No! It's a ghost!" Frantically he began to wave his hands to the other men pointing into the darkness. Having caught their attention the men drew closer to the side of the boat wiping the water from their eyes hoping to get a glimpse.

"I see it! It has to be a ghost!" one yelled. Each one began to cry out in terror at the figure walking among the giant waves. Their shrieks pierced through the roar of the wind.

The figure on the water cried out, "Take courage! I am! Stop being afraid!"

Their thoughts raced, *Was that the voice of Jesus? It sounds like Him.*

Peter cried out, "Lord, if it is You, command me to come to You on the water!"

"Come!" Jesus yelled back from the dark.

Peter was trembling with excitement that Jesus had come. Without a thought he scrambled over the edge of the boat keeping his eye on Jesus. He didn't want to lose sight of Him. As his feet landed in the water the waves lashed at him but they did not take him down. He was standing on water. His feet began to move toward Jesus. Suddenly, his realized that the waves were thrashing all around him while the strong wind pushed hard against his body. He couldn't see anything else now. Right away he could feel the water rising around him as he began to sink into its depths.

"Lord, save me!" Peter cried as the water began to swallow his head.

Peter could hear the water filling his ears muting the sound from above. Instantly He could feel a firm grip upon his out stretched hand. Jesus began to pull him up above the water drawing him beside Him.

Jesus spoke into Peter's ear, "O you of little faith, why did you doubt?"

Leaning into the shoulder of Jesus, Peter wondered how he could have doubted when it was Jesus who had told him to come. Jesus wouldn't have told him to come if He wasn't going to take care of him. The waves became his focus instead of keeping his eyes on Jesus.

Gripping Jesus' hand even tighter sent peace surging through his body, calming him. It was as if he had become oblivious to the storm around him as it stood in attention to God's peace. It all seemed surreal. The raging wind was no longer an issue. All he could see was Jesus who had saved him. No longer could Peter rely on his experience of prior storms and knowing people who had died at sea. He would put his trust in Jesus Who had rescued him from death.

Having reached the boat they crawled over its side putting the solid wood floor beneath their feet. As soon as their feet touched the floor of the boat the storm came to an abrupt halt. The boat no longer reeled in the waves but had come to a steady rocking.

In response to the obvious authority of Jesus every man fell on their knees crying out, "Truly You are the Son of God!" (Matt 14: 22-33). No other man could have walked on water and have a storm obey like that. One moment they were afraid for their life and in the next they were safe because of Jesus. At that moment they knew they could fully trust Jesus, the Truth, who came to restore mankind back to the Father. (Malachi 4:5,6).

Jesus as Truth came to restore trust in God the Father. Truth and trust brings us into relationship with God. Then why do we today lack trust? Too often distrust has become the rapid response to one another. Many find it hard to trust family, government, bosses, employees, the church and even God.

Trust is the fruit of truth. If we lack trust then maybe we aren't connected with real truth? Mankind is always in search of truth. It is man's inherent need for truth that compels him to keep seeking it. While apart from God, mankind thinks they have found truth within some manmade dead religion or a philosophical reasoning based on man's opinion. Truth cannot be found apart from God.

Truth creates trust and a lie produces distrust. Lies keep us from truth just as they did Adam and Eve. What lies are we believing that keep us from the truth?

We find too many churches distrusting people and other denominations. Why such a lack of trust? Could this be because our theology is watered down truth rooted in methods of self-effort? Distrust is the litmus test that we may have formed a doctrine outside God's complete truth. What if we can't find trust because we only trust ourselves? We may have believed a lie about God and Truth.

Jesus said He is "the Way, the Truth and the Life." (John 14:6). He is the way to truth because He is Truth embodied. It can only be found in Him. When we are rooted in Jesus, the Truth, trusting Him will become a natural element in our lives.

The gut wrenching sobs echoed off the rocky cliffs surrounding the crowd, intently watching Jesus, bent over, heaving in deep groans. Tears oozed past the tightly clad fingers covering His eyes as His forehead met the dirt below.

You could hear the whispers being raised among the crowd, "See how He loved Lazarus!"; "Surely if He could open blind eyes couldn't He have prevented this man from dying?"; "Where was He before he died?"

Jesus leaned back on His heels, lifting His face upward with a resounding moan. Slowly staggering to His feet He turned toward the cave where Lazarus had been laid. Clearing His throat and wiping away the tears He turned to Martha. As He motioned toward the tomb He spoke hoarsely, "Take away the stone".

The last bit of color drained from Martha's face as her mouth dropped open in dismay. Haltingly, she exclaimed, "But Lord, by this time his body is already decaying! It has been four days. If you open that tomb it will stink!"

Martha's mind raced over the events of the previous week. She had sent a message to Jesus when Lazarus became ill. He didn't come. Moment after moment she watched for Jesus to walk through the door but to no avail. Why hadn't He come when we asked Him too? If he had we wouldn't be standing here right now.

Jesus' eyes glistened as He stared unwaveringly into her eyes and He whispered, "Did I not tell you that if you believe on Me, you would see the glory of God?"

As Martha gazed into those love filled eyes the anguish of His not coming faded away. How many times had she been a firsthand witness of miracle after miracle performed by Jesus? Played out before her eyes was a relentless compassion like no other she had ever seen. She couldn't remember ever being let down by Him. Without breaking her gaze she motioned for someone to roll away the stone from the cave entrance.

Lifting His eyes He spoke, "Father, I thank You that You have heard Me. Yes, I know You always hear Me, but I have said this for the benefit of the people standing around, so that they may believe that You did send Me".

Setting His eyes on the gaping black hole He shouted in a loud voice, "Lazarus, come out!"

Time stood still as everyone silently stared at the cave opening. Gasps escaped every mouth as the man who had been dead walked out, wrapped from head to toe in burial clothes.

Jesus said, "Free him of the burial wrappings and let him go".

Many in the crowd began to draw back frantically whispering among themselves. A hushed awe filled the atmosphere as the people grappled to understand what had just transpired. Many Jews believed in Jesus that day.

Rushing forward Martha wrapped Lazarus in her arms sobbing with joy. Her thoughts raced, *Oh why did I think it was too late? Why did I not trust Jesus and know He was always faithful?* (John 11: 1-45).

Martha stepped into a deeper trust that day in Jesus, the Truth. No matter the circumstance…no matter the outcome…Jesus can be trusted completely. She learned to not question, but only believe.

When we live fully trusting in God we then abide in God's peace, knowing all is well. It is a position Adam and Eve had once known, before truth was discarded, but Jesus (Ephesians 4:21) restored trust through His becoming Truth.

The position of trust can come into its fullness when we lower ourselves into the lap of Christ Jesus and rest in His Truth.

The Truth About Humility

Jesus is the essence of true humility. He told parables about it and displayed it over and over again. Even though Jesus demonstrated humility, do we truly comprehend what he wanted us to see? Could we possibly misunderstand what humility is? Too often today's concept of humility is eclipsed by a "false" humility. This false humility leads us into believing we are being humble, but basically we're missing the point. We can find the answer to these questions by looking at the only person to ever walk in the fullness of true humility...Jesus.

The grass tore at his fingers as He methodically braided the strands together. To build the whip long enough He had to add stem after stem to the braid. His fingers worked effortlessly from years of making rope. Jesus had learned this basic skill from Joseph, His earthly father.

His thoughts raced, *How far His people had removed themselves from the Father's heart. God's house had become a source of private gain which played upon people's drive to follow the prescribed rules. There is no escape from the self-made laws of the Synagogue leaders.* He could feel the frustration boiling inside at the greed that dispelled the true purpose of His Father's house; a place to connect people with Himself. *It was the deceitful hearts of man taking advantage of a people who didn't know any better. The function of the temple had become a merchandizing den of the things of God.*

Strands of hair kept escaping from behind His ear threatening to hide His task. In one smooth move He swept the hair back into place as His fingers returned to braiding the whip. The sound of people going about their daily schedules hovered in the background of His thoughts. Time was closing in as the merchants finished laying their wares out in the temple square. Ringing between the stone walls were the coo of doves in their cages, the bleats of sheep and heavy hooves of the oxen pounding on the ground as they were herded into their stalls. Rising above the clatter of the people He could hear the merchants beginning to yell out their prices, compelling the people to come buy.

As He secured the end of the last piece of grass He swiftly looked up at the crowds that were beginning to gather to make their purchases for their offerings they were about to present. He ran the rope through His hands, checking its strength and length. This should serve its purpose.

He could feel His stomach flutter as He rose to His feet. It was only just a few days ago He had performed His first miracle as the Son of man. He could still hear the people's word's of awe as He and His mother left at the end of the wedding. As He looked into their eyes He could see a faint hope peering out of the weariness they wore. It caused His heart to ache because of their lost, isolated position from their Father God. Taking in a deep breath and releasing it He whispered, "I Am their hope! I have come to set them free. We have longed for this day since the creation of the world."

Standing in the middle of the vending area He eyed each table displaying its wares. Close to the owner's tables were small stalls crammed with sheep and oxen fidgeting in their tight quarters. Cages of doves were stacked against the stalls. He could smell the hay and manure as He inhaled the air.

The flame of His heart for mankind exploded into a raging fire as He screamed, "Ahhh!" With the swing of His arm His whip began to scrape across the tables sending the wares flying through the air. The whip doubled back sending the money jars crashing to the ground. In the same rhythm the fingers on His other hand caught the edge of the table tipping it over in one orchestrated move. Turning quickly his foot smashed into the makeshift stall sending it flying as the animals bolted in fear. Bodies were exiting to the left and right as they dodged the snap of the whip. Like a whirlwind He tore through all the merchandiser's tables, focused on the wares being sold.

Halting in front of a stall selling doves He shouted, "Take these things away! Make not My Father's house a house of merchandising!" (John 2:14-17). His body trembled as His rushing emotions exploded for the freedom of His people and the pilfering of His Father's character. It was this merchandizing before Him that separated God and His people. How He hated anything that separated them. After all, they had been separated long enough. Sweat poured down His face as His clothes clung to His drenched body.

Amazingly the large crowd shrank back in silence. The occasional whispers arose, "He's mad!, Who does He think He is? Why would He go on such a rampage?" The clouds of dust began to clear as some began to crawl on the ground searching for their coins.

Out of breath He stood motionless. With the attention of all He yelled, "No more merchandizing in my Father's house!" Quietly He walked away as people followed in curiosity at such a man. (John 2: 14-16).

If Jesus is humility itself then how can this kind of action be categorized as humble? At least not the way we have been taught about humility. How does His own teaching of "turning the other cheek" fit into the display of these actions? Jesus was the only man to walk completely humble, yet He turned the money changers tables over and purposefully made a whip to drive them out. Maybe there is something we are missing when it comes to being humble.

There it was again! Sara was being told she needed to back down while she was being treated rudely by another Christian. She was told for the umpteenth time over the preceding years, "They are allowing us to use their building for free and we need to be grateful. We need to show them more often how grateful we are. We have to show them love."

Sara's answer was always about the same, "I am not ungrateful! We have given them cards, bought supplies and we have jumped to their ever growing demands about the use of their building. In so many words we've been accused of walking away with items in the building. There is something wrong when a professing Christian can be so negative and accusing most of the time." Frustration had grown to an all time high. The rest of the team didn't have these accusations hurled at them personally like Sara and her husband had. But, then they were the leaders and things like that come with the territory. She spent far too much time feeling condemned. It always appeared that maybe she wasn't being humble enough because she didn't always feel like "turning the other cheek" or "going the extra mile".

Their team's unrealistic approach as to what humility was became a frustration to her because they couldn't really even discuss the situation. It seemed by discussing the problem she wasn't being grateful or humble…she was being negative. Her heart's desire was not to be negative and she was very grateful for their generosity. But there was a real problem with how they were being treated and she was tired of it. The knot in the pit of her stomach said this isn't how humility works. They didn't have be a doormat.

Sara began to seek God as to what must be wrong with her. Was she not being humble? What should her reaction be to this kind of behavior towards them? She was ready to repent if need be. What was missing from this picture?

The story about Sara represents a revelation God showed me about how the church views *humility*. For a number of years God had been teaching me about rest and how we can't move in our own wisdom but only in what God is saying and doing. It was out of this teaching God showed me where true humility sprang from…rest.

God used the story about Jesus overturning the tables to show me about true humility. He was one worked up guy! He looked far from humble according to our definition, but He could respond like that because He was truly humble. His humility was born out of His position of rest in the Father. His soul was anchored in God and did not master His spirit. He only said and did what the Father told Him. Jesus did not please Himself or receive honor from any man, but only from God the Father. This is how he could be humble and overturn the tables in the synagogue.

Being humble isn't about not responding to people's attacks...though that's what we've been led to believe. It is about being at rest in the Father and only doing and saying what He says. Jesus heard the Father say, "turn the other cheek" as He was being crucified upon the cross. But He also heard the Father say, "Overturn the tables in the synagogue" and He did it in true humility. He also heard the Father tell Him to not let the Pharisee's get away with their religious ways. He was in their face all the way to the cross, in humility.

Humility is *not* walking in the ways of the flesh but in the ways of the Spirit of God. We can actually turn the other cheek and really be walking in the flesh - even though it looks like a Godly thing to do...being in the Bible and all. But then it would qualify as doing things according to what you *do* instead of *being* in Christ Jesus at rest.

False humility is when you do things according to how you think it should be done, just because it looks humble in the religious community. The greater point is missed; only doing what the Father is doing. One day God might say go the extra mile by forgiving someone who wronged you. Another day He might say I want you to not allow that person to get away with doing you that way. All of it can be done in love because it will be the direction of the Holy Spirit. When we allow Holy Spirit that kind of control in our lives we cannot help but love no matter what we are directed to do.

When the church begins to understand true humility we will be a church who knows our authority in Christ. We will be a people who will not back down, but yet ones who know when to turn the other cheek.

The way to true humility is the path of lower placing all our actions in Him as He leads us into the best way to respond.

Covered

Adam and Eve began life covered by God through His Spirit, but with their fall they stepped out from under God's covering leaving them bare. Just as Adam and Eve found makeshift covers, so we too attempt to cover ourselves through self-effort.

The tree of the knowledge represented God's wisdom and truth; only He has all knowledge. Adam and Eve were not to eat of the tree of knowledge because God's truth, His knowledge, kept them anchored safely in Him. They could rest under the cover of the tree's branches knowing God's truth was keeping them safe. They were covered in Him.

Adam and Eve were created in His image; spirit, soul and body. It was their spirit which hosted their body...it covered them completely. The spirit was in direct connection with God and had rule over the soul. When they chose to eat of the tree of knowledge their soul man became the ruler; a free agent. They were left vulnerable without the spirit's cover. Death was quickly realized as their spirit man was replaced by the soul man. They were no longer led by the spirit but by their self-will and judgments. They were left naked and bare. Knowing the dilemma sin had left them in God provided a temporary cover until Jesus provided the final cover.

All Adam and Eve had ever known was being covered by their spirit. Now that this cover was gone their bodies were now unprotected from the elements of a now fallen world. To protect them God made skin and wrapped it around their exposed bodies. Most traditional teaching says that God performed the first sacrifice by slaying an animal to use its skin as a cover for Adam and Eve. When looking closer at the Hebrew words nowhere does it mention God using animal skins. In fact, no animal is even mentioned in that scripture. It says He made long coats of skin and wrapped it around them. (Gen 3:21). At this time God created skin and it became the bodies covering. Skin covering them was something new because all they had known was to be covered with the spirit. Science verifies God's purpose for skin by stating that it protects the body from the elements of the world and helps regulate body temperature, and permits the sensations of touch, heat, and cold.

But, it was only a temporary fix. Man was still in need of the life of the spirit to rule the flesh. They were wrapped in the confines of flesh where the soul now ruled. Living by the dictates of the flesh keeps mankind separated from an intimate relationship with the Father.

Jesus came to reestablish the truth of man's origin by laying down His self-will and nailing the flesh to the cross which anchored us back into the Father. He said, "I am the Way, the Truth and the Life." His blood was spilled out, washing over us to make us clean and restoring mankind to their rightful place. Mankind was once again connected to God through Jesus' life blood. Our spirit is now once again made alive, covering us as one made in God's image; spirit beings not flesh beings.

Yet, even though Jesus has now made us alive in our spirit most often we don't live in the reality of that fact. We remain swathed in the same lie that Adam and Eve were duped by. Satan continues his lies, making us believe we are left naked and it nudges us to wrap ourselves with our fleshly works instead of the spirit. What we think has covered us has actually caused us to hide behind our makeshift fig leaves of self preservation. Our soul rules us more than we realize.

In living this soul ruled life, we judge others in an attempt to protect ourselves. Our criticisms are deemed as truth because we believe our perspective is fact. Unknowingly, our criticisms become fig leaves to hide the intent of our heart. No wonder there is so much discord...we all think we are right.

We must look at Jesus' response with others to understand how we should react. In the Gospel of John, chapter eight we are told about a woman caught in adultery. Jesus did not judge the situation from law's standpoint. Instead, He made a garment of the Father's love covering her shame and exposing the hearts of those accusing her. Choosing the Father's perspective He could rightly respond from the Father's heart.

The stinging slap jolted her awake. As she struggled to focus her eyes, the pain crept across her face leaving an aching numbness. Staring back at the figure towering over her she realized the room was full of other men peering at her. Frantically she began to pull the blanket over her naked body.

Her mind raced, *What is going on? Why is he doing this*? The night had begun like most nights with some man's payment for a turn in her bed. It was no surprise for a Pharisee leader to come knocking at her door in the dark of night for his selfish satisfaction. The man standing over her came often. Before she fell asleep he was already fast asleep beside her. Now, fully clothed he grabbed her arm as he began pulling her out of bed yelling, "You, wicked women! You are going to be stoned for this!" The other men stared at her as they pressed in around him yelling their own accusations. Barely grabbing the blanket her fingers fumbled as she covered herself the best she could.

This wasn't at all what she had wanted for her life. But then, there weren't many options for women whose husband's chose to fabricate lies so they could divorce them. Women had no rights in the courts. They were considered of less worth than the animals…possessions to discard at will. At first it was hard selling her body, but it became easier as numbness captured her soul. The days would fade into each other, forming endless days of nonexistence.

The cool morning breeze hit her sweat drenched body as the men drug her through the streets. She ashamedly endeavored to hide her face and body from the stares of the people gathering to see what the ruckus was all about. Beneath her bare feet the stone pavement sent shivers through her bones. The further they went the bigger the crowd grew around her. The grip of the hands pulling her along made her arms throb.

Where are they taking me? If they take me before the Sanhedrin it could mean death! her mind raced. It seemed time had stood still as fear gripped her, draining any remaining strength. She desperately tried catching her breath as panic forced her throat shut.

They broke through into the temple courtyard crowded with people. Crashing through the group they moved toward a man at the center. Thrusting her toward the man she tumbled to the ground at his feet. The wet hair clinging to her face kept her from seeing who they had thrust her before. She could feel pain in her knees and hands from skidding across the hard dirt. In the wake of the pain she frantically gathered and tucked the blanket close around her as she lowered her face in shame. She could feel the hatred of the men's eyes burning into her back. All she wanted was to disappear.

The hands grabbed her again as they yanked her to her feet. Roughly they turned her towards the man loudly saying, "Teacher, this woman has been caught in the very act of adultery. Now Moses in the Law commanded us that such shall be stoned to death. But what do you say?"

Silence met the question. She quickly brushed the hair out of her eyes so she could see who she stood in front of.

He had bent down writing in the dirt with his finger. He wasn't like the other men. Curiosity began to override the fear.

"Teacher, this woman has been caught in adultery. Our law says she must be stoned, but what do you say?" they repeated. He continued writing in the dirt seemingly oblivious to the question. Again they repeated the ignored question with agitation rising in their voice.

Slowly He rose to His feet and said, "Let him who is without sin among you be the first to throw a stone at her". Then He bent down again to write in the dirt with His finger. His silence permeated the crowd.

She couldn't believe that this man had not come into agreement with the Pharisee's. Hope fluttered in the pit of her stomach. The sound of a rock falling and shuffling feet pulled her eyes around to see one of the men leaving the crowd with his head bent low. Amazingly, another man dropped his rock as he followed suit and then another and another until the last accuser had left.

Now, she was the only one standing in the center surrounded by scattered rocks. The man quit writing and stood up and said, "Woman, where are your accusers? Has no man condemned you?"

As she raised her head her eyes were captured by the beauty of the man's eyes. She had never seen such love in anyone's eyes. They seemed to reach down into the depth of her soul leaving a spark of hope that even she could be clean again.

"No one, Lord!" she gasped.

"I do not condemn you either. Go on your way and from now on sin no more." He whispered as His eyes burned into her heart.

Wrapping the blanket tightly around her she realized that amazingly she didn't feel so naked anymore. She couldn't understand what had transpired. Never had she met such compassion. As she walked away she whispered to herself, "I must find out who this man is. He seems to have power over the Pharisee's. No one dared to address them the way He did". (John 8: 1-11).

Jesus made a covering, a garment as it were, for her nakedness so the men could no longer accuse her. He literally wrapped her in His love leaving her accusers laid bare where they could hide no longer from their own sins. It was her guilt they used to cover their own sinful actions.

Jesus told the parable about a King saying, "…when I was naked you clothed me…You did this when you clothed others" (Matthew 25:36-44). He wasn't only talking about physical clothing. Spiritual clothing can also be assembled to cover people's shame or downfall. Jesus knew the woman was living in sin but He also understood the men were using her to trick Him and were diverting their own sin by highlighting hers.

The garment Jesus made protected her from the judgment of others. So also we need to make garments for those who are caught in their sin. Does that mean we ignore sin? No, but through our not condemning we wrap people in a garment of love that guides them to the Father. By not joining the judgment competition we make protective garments and it silences the accusers.

Peter said that, "Love covers a multitude of sins." (1 Peter 4:8). If Jesus used His love to cover the woman caught in adultery then we too can make a garment of love to hide the sins of people so they can be restored.

By doing this we do not give our own sinful criticism a place to hide. When we make garments for others we also keep our heart clean before God by not leaving anything in our lives that the enemy can use against us. We actually live behind the garment that Jesus has made for each one of us; wrapped in His forgiveness.

As we cover others in the love of Jesus scripture says we will be "blessed" and our "sins are covered". (Romans 4:7). We are then declaring the truth God speaks about them and ourselves…the truth of our identity in Him. When we cover others it enlarges our heart to function as God's heart.

So, what do we do the next time our spouse or children argue about their differing opinions or as they get angry? Make a garment of God's grace. What about the co-worker or church member that is the constant irritant? Make a garment of God's love to cover. Or the homeless person or those caught in addiction? Make a garment of God's hope. As you do this God's love will begin to grow while bringing change to your heart and it will flow out upon others.

Removing the soul's cover positions us to receive God's covering, which is the only wrap that truly covers.

Go ahead make those garments and you will find that it will cover your life too. The focus comes off of you and brings you to a place of lower in Him.

5 By the Spirit

Human Point of View

The way lower is to head downward - away from being lifted up in our own understanding. As we allow our mind to be renewed to think like Jesus we begin to see others differently…that is from a different point of view.

Jesus "died for all, so that all those who live might live no longer to and for *themselves*" but "for Him who died and was raised again for their sake." (2 Cor 5:15). We are to actually "… regard no one from a human point of view" (2 Cor 5:16) but from a spirit viewpoint. Just as we now see Jesus in His resurrected body we are to see others "in Christ" as a "new creation" where their "old has passed away" and their "new has come!" (2 Cor 5:17). We have to see each other as ones who are "from God" whom "Jesus reconciled" back "to Himself". (2 Cor 5:18). When we look at one another we need to see through our spirit eyes. As we begin to do this we will begin to be transformed from the dictate of our human point of view into God's viewpoint. Jesus exemplified this concept.

Her feet sailed across the wide trodden path. She had traveled this direction many times and her feet remembered each step. Likewise, the path had delivered many generations of people to Jacob's well for their water supply. The empty water jars balanced easily on each of her shoulders. It was the trip back, when the jars were full, that were harder to hold and balance. Intentionally arriving long after most had drawn their water saved her from any accusing stares.

Stopping short when the well came into view she noticed a Man sitting alone by the well. She hadn't seen Him around before.

Great! she thought. *He's a Jew. I'll quickly get my water and He will probably, like most Jewish men, ignore me.*

Approaching as far away as she could, she shifted her jars to the ground. Her eyes stayed focused on unwinding the rope that would lower her jars into the water. She could feel the mid-day sun penetrating through her outer wrap.

"Give Me a drink," the Man blurted out.

Complete dismay swept over her as she processed His words. *Jewish men do not speak to women much less to a Samaritan woman! What is His real motive?*

"You, being a Jew, ask me, a Samaritan woman, for a drink?" spilled her words as her hand shielded the sun to get a better look at the Man speaking. Her quick tongue had gotten herself into trouble most of her life. So why would this time be any different?

With a smile lurking at the corner of His mouth He said, "If you had only known and had recognized God's gift and Who this is that is saying to you, 'Give Me a drink,' you would have asked Him instead and he would have given you living water."

She stood there staring as she tried to keep her mouth from dropping open. Her thoughts raced, *What is this guy talking about? His words make no sense.*

Her eyes swept Him from head to toe as she hesitantly said, "Sir, You have nothing to draw with and the well is deep; how then can You provide living water?" She continued as her words mocked, "Are You greater than our ancestor Jacob, who gave us this well and who used to drink from it himself, and his sons and his cattle?"

The Man continued, obviously ignoring the intent of her words, "All who drink of this water will be thirsty again. But whoever takes a drink of the water that I will give him shall never, no never, be thirsty any more. But the water that I will give him shall become a spring of water welling up within him unto eternal life."

Wonder and a tinge of excitement began to flutter inside her. What He was saying made no sense, but there was something about Him that drew her. As she stared into the most loving eyes she had ever seen she felt that somehow His words were true. His words tugged at the emptiness inside. Many times she wished her life had turned out differently, but she felt trapped by her own actions and by the title many had pinned upon her.

Slowly the words floated from her lips, "Sir, give me this water, so that I may never get thirsty nor have to come here to draw".

"Go, call your husband and come back here," He said.

Her back stiffened at the statement. Looking away she tugged at the rope in her hand. Cautiously she said, "I have no husband."

"You have spoken truly in saying, "I have no husband." His eyes danced with amusement as He continued, "For you have had five husbands and the man you are now living with is not your husband. In this you have spoken truly."

She jerked her eyes back upon the Man as He stood to His feet. As He walked toward her a cold shockwave jolted through her body as her thoughts raced, *I have never seen this Man before so how does He know this? Is He trying to show me He is better than me?* The shame of her life obviously couldn't be kept from Him. Taking a step back, her cocky words spilled from her mouth toward the Man, "Sir, I see that You are a prophet. Our forefathers worshiped on this mountain, but you Jews say that Jerusalem is the place where it is proper to worship."

"Woman, believe Me, a time is coming when you will worship the Father neither in this mountain nor in Jerusalem," the man said.

Her thoughts tumbled as He effectively tossed out the argument that had gone on for generations. He was obviously a Jew but yet He presented a whole new thought she had never heard before.

Gesturing with His hands He continued, "You Samaritans do not know what you are worshiping. We do know what we are worshiping, for salvation comes from the Jews. A time will come, however, indeed it is already here, when the true worshipers will worship the Father in spirit and in truth; for the Father is seeking just such people as these as His worshipers. God is a Spirit and those who worship Him must worship Him in spirit and truth."

Knowing His words were true about salvation coming through the Jews she said, "I know that Messiah is coming, He Who is called the Christ; and when He arrives, He will tell us everything we need to know and will make it clear to us."

The Man leaned in closer as His eyes tenderly locked onto hers as He whispered, "I Who now speak with you am He." An unseen power penetrated from His words.

A gasp escaped her mouth as her shocked eyes stared deeply into His. The understanding of His words swept through her heart. In an instant she knew what He said was true. The approaching steps and voices couldn't pull her gaze from the face of Messiah standing before her. Hope was beginning to fill her heart; a feeling that had long been absent. She was amazed that He would take time to talk to her, a shamed Samaritan woman.

Little did she know that the approaching group of men were appalled that the Messiah was talking to a Samaritan woman. Anyway, at this point, even if she had known it wouldn't have mattered because she had just experienced the acceptance of the Messiah. He had chosen to talk to her even though He knew all about her life. Excitedly she thought, "People have to know that the Christ has come." Quickly she left the water jars and ran into town to tell the people that the Messiah had come. (John 4: 4-28).

This story is only one of many examples where Jesus did not look at the people from His "human" point of view. He looked at the heart of the people no matter what their sins were, no matter what they had done wrong. All He knew was that He wanted them to be reconciled with the Father. Before He had even talked to the Samaritan woman He knew all the wrong things she was doing; yet, He still chose to present Himself to her. Also, He defied the traditional "view point" of the Jews to stay away from Samaritans…especially Samaritan women. By choosing to only see this woman through His spiritual eyes He was able to break down the judgments of what people thought of others. He only addressed the gold He had placed within.

We too, like Jesus, should only respond to one another from spiritual, God given eyes. What gold are we missing when we interact with people each day? Are our judgments and criticisms keeping people from the value the Father has placed upon them through our devaluing opinion? Do their wrongs keep the Father from seeking them out? No. Then neither should we look at people from a "human point of view". Putting on our spiritual eyes, the eyes of the Father, will allow us to bring people into the loving kindness and forgiveness that Jesus holds for all mankind.

It will then release people from the bondage of rejection. Not to mention it also releases us from the bondage of relying on our own wisdom.

When we see with spiritual eyes it allows us to begin to live in the life of lower where we do not exalt our own judgments and opinions, but lift others up toward the Father. It is the journey of lower.

Jesus, knowing the flaw of man's viewpoint, knew not to entrust Himself to them. (John 2:24). This helped Him to not be taken in by all the arguments the Pharisees' assailed against Him. He knew their viewpoint was only their fleshly opinion. By not listening to what they thought of Him kept His mind directed on His mission.

It was very important that He didn't engage in the opinion of those railing against Him. But even more importantly He did not entrust Himself to the viewpoint of those who revered Him as man. He didn't allow their desire to place His man-form up on a pedestal of human worship to fill Him with pride. He did not entrust Himself to man's opinion which is the way lower in order to be lifted up by God not by man.

In like manner we can't be moved by the viewpoint of man. Even when they attack us or place us on top of a pedestal we can't be moved by their opinion of us. This is where we go lower, going as far away from entrusting ourselves to man's viewpoint or even relying on our own fleshly viewpoint. Only by being led by the Spirit can we truly have a correct understanding; a heavenly view with no flesh touching it.

We've got to lower our fleshly understanding and take on God's higher way of thought so we can be all that God has called us to be.

Spirit Eyes

Having spiritual eyes is imperative for sons of God. Adam and Eve had spiritual eyes before they traded them for eyes of the flesh. Jesus won back those spirit eyes for his body to use once again. Fear has permeated the church of anything that steps outside the realm of the seen world. The voices of human reasoning warn against anything connected to the spirit world because they fear the demons that might rule there and fear falling into their trap.

How can we fear the spirit realm since God is Spirit? He breathed His breath into Adam giving him His Spirit. Anything connected to the spirit is God's and those that are His. The only reason the demons have rule in this realm is that we, as sons of God, have not occupied that realm. To live as mature sons we must take this realm back by bringing God's heavenly kingdom to earth.

Gehazi had been tossing and turning in his bed for most of the night. He couldn't get his mind off what the messenger had to say when he came to the gate of the city the day before. The King of Syria had given orders to seize his master, Elisha, at all cost.

He had the privilege to serve Elisha, a prophet of God, for many years now. God had been telling Elisha the very words the King of Syria had been speaking privately to his captains of their strategy against Israel. Elisha had been sharing what he heard with the King of Israel. Time after time Israel was side stepping Syria's well laid plans. The King of Syria was livid with anger when he was informed that it was Elisha who was revealing their secrets to Israel.

How could they escape a king that was bent on destroying them? This king was known for his relentless pursuit of his target. Different scenarios ran through his mind of how they could escape. None of them seemed to ease the fear that was building within him.

The dark of the night was just beginning to be transformed from pitch black. Gehazi flung back the covers tired of the fight for sleep. He had to move; his body was aching from the disturbed night.

Squinting into the haze of morning he stepped out onto the balcony where the cool air began to rouse him awake. He jumped as he barely missed the figure standing next to the railing. Peering closer he could see it was Elisha staring up at the surrounding mountains. Following his gaze Gehazi's heart sank. There were night torches glowing across the mountain. A cold shiver shot down Gehazi's back as he whispered, "This has to be the King of Syria! They have found us! What shall we do master?"

Without moving a muscle Elisha calmly stated, "Fear not; for those with us are more than those with them."

Gehazi's head jerked to look at Elisha. His thoughts raced, There *are only two of us and how many people in this city would defend them? I don't see them standing with weapons to help us. How could he be so calm? We are surrounded by an army that is focused on capturing this one man. Since I am his servant what will they do to me?* He lowered his head into his hands wearily saying, "What are we going to do?"

Elisha's hands shot upward as Gehazi's head jolted up looking at him in surprise. Elisha's voice boomed out, "Lord, I pray You open his eyes that he may see!"

Immediately the torch lights of the Syrian's faded behind a host of angels seated on horses and chariots. The mountain was filled with angels. Why couldn't he see this before? The horse's feet were stamping as their bodies swayed with excitement. The angels were waving their swords in great anticipation. He could now see that the "more" that was with them was an army of angels hidden from his natural sight. The Syrian army was surrounded by angels but yet they were clueless of their presence.

His mouth dropped at the sight before him. Hope rose up within him as he wondered, *Why did I doubt? God has always taken care of us.* (2 Kings 6:15-17).

What kept Gehazi from seeing what Elisha was seeing? He was looking from his natural eyes instead of his spiritual eyes. We will probably one day be surprised when we learn of all the times this was the case with us, where we were clueless because we had not trained our spiritual eyes to see the truth of what was surrounding us.

We become tied into what our natural eye perceives more than we realize. What we don't grasp is that when we gratify the appetites and impulses of the flesh we cannot be in agreement with God (Rom 8:8) and His spirit realm. This actually puts us in opposition to God, for our fleshly mind does not submit itself to God. (Rom 8:7). Often we miss what is going on in the spirit realm because we haven't learned to separate ourselves from our fleshly sight.

Romans 8:13 states that "If you live according to the flesh, you will surely die. But if through the power of the Spirit you are putting to death the practice of the body (the flesh), you shall live." When we live from what we see through our natural eye it brings us death because we were created as spiritual beings. The scripture says that, "For all who are led by the Spirit of God are sons of God." (Rom 8:14). Having spiritual eyes like Elisha displays our sonship. Yet many of us, like Gehazi, only engage in the natural realm and are often clueless about the spirit realm.

Spiritual eyes are the key to stepping into the authority given us as sons of God. We have been mandated to take the gospel into the entire world and reconcile it back to God; bringing heaven to earth. The earth literally groans for the sons of God to be made known. (Rom 8:19). We, as spirit sons, are the earth's hope of restoration. Even the earth knows we are not functioning in our capacity. It knows we are still relying on our fleshly eyes instead of our spiritual eyes. The bondage and decay will cease when the true sons begin to walk as a unit separated from the natural world.

When we put our focus on a particular thing we actually come into agreement with what we engage in. So if we focus on the natural world we come into agreement with a world that is in bondage to the destructive fall of Adam and Eve. No wonder we don't walk victoriously because we are in agreement with the very thing that we are trying to overcome. We become what we behold and we possess what we see.

Sowing into fleshly things will cause us to reap the carnal things. But, if we sow into the spirit we will reap the life that the spirit brings. (Gal 6:8). What do you want to reap? Things of this world or things in the spirit where there is life? We need to begin to sow accordingly. To walk in the spirit we must break our agreement with fleshly things so we can bring life back to the earth.

Jesus pointed us toward the spirit realm over and over again to move us out of the natural into the supernatural. He did this by walking on water, turning water into wine, raising the dead, cloaking Himself as He walked unseen through the crowds, healing the sick and casting out demons; all of it requires functioning in the spirit realm pulling it into what is seen. He only did what He saw the Father doing through using His spirit eyes. Yet he did all this while functioning fully as man. He showed us what is attainable as a man living with spirit eyes.

If we walk in the spirit then we will not fulfill the desires of the flesh. (Gal 5:16). This gives us the power to overcome as we display God's character which is the fruit of the spirit. (Gal 5:22). This fruit can only be obtained through keeping our focus on the realm of the spirit and not on the natural world. We would then bring the light of God upon the natural world, dispelling its darkness.

Many times Peter, James and John walked the well beaten path up into the mountain with Jesus to pray. This time Jesus only wanted to take a few of His disciples with Him. Peter could feel excitement rising in him with each step. He felt so alive when he was around Jesus. These special times when he was asked to go pray made him feel there was a greater purpose to his life other than fishing. Often he felt like he was on the brink of explosion with all the emotions boiling within him. Some would call it impulsive, others might call it anger. Either way he often acted before his thoughts engaged. "I hate how that always seems to happen! I really need to work on that," he thought. "But, I don't know what to do with all these volatile emotions pent-up inside."

The men were laughing and teasing one another as they hiked the trail. This is the kind of thing that made Peter feel so connected with these men; he could be himself. They had in many ways become his family.

Jesus was stopping at their usual place. Everyone began finding a comfortable spot to land with their bags and blanket. They would be here all night praying.

It had become dark after praying for quite some time. Peter's back was beginning to ache from standing and sitting so long. He laid down on his blanket with a rock to support his head. Immediately the pain began to subside as his muscles began to relax.

He began to think about the events of last week. Jesus' coming had answered a number of questions many had about God, but there seemed to be even more questions raised the longer they were around Jesus.

After Jesus had miraculously multiplied the loaves of bread and the fish He told them to not tell anyone who He really was and that He was going to be put to death and be raised up again. The words seemed to cramp his brain! What did He mean? Jesus is the Messiah, He can't die, because He is supposed to save them from the Romans and become their King.

There was one puzzling statement Jesus made, "I tell you truly, there are some of those standing here who will not taste death before they see the kingdom of God." Now that statement scrambled his brain! Jesus talked a lot about God's kingdom, but there seemed to be something further he wasn't grasping about it. Not taste death? Did He mean there were some who would not die? These thoughts began to fade away as Peter drifted to sleep.

The sound of the others moving around him began to awaken him. As he started opening his eyes a glaring bright light caused him to blink. His hand shot up over his eyes shading them so he could see where the light was coming from. Next to him James and John were also trying to make out where the source of light came from. Looking in the direction of the light he caught sight of Jesus standing there talking to two other men. Their bodies and clothing were lit up brighter than he had ever seen; they were glowing from head to toe.

The groggy disciples caught the drifting words of the men, "The plan of your Father will soon be revealed as you give yourself over to death. Soon you will be back with your Father." Jesus bowed His head as he said, "Yes, Moses and Elijah, this is the day you had hoped to see so long ago. Soon I will be reconciling all men back to God! Death to my flesh will put all men's flesh to death once for all. I pray my disciple's will rise up in the victory I am winning for them."

Peter's thoughts raced as he heard them talking about Jesus exiting this world. *He's talking to Moses and Elijah? How could that be? They were dead…weren't they?* But they were standing before him.

As usual Peter spoke without thinking about what he was saying, "Jesus, Master, it is delightful that we are here; let us construct three booths - one for You and one for Moses and one for Elijah!"

While he was still speaking a cloud overshadowed them. Fear struck them as the cloud enclosed around them. A voice came out of the cloud saying, "This is My Son, My Beloved; listen to Him!" Peter, James and John fell on their faces unable to move.

Peter feeling a hand on his shoulder turned to see who touched him. It was Jesus. He was back to His normal self. Moses and Elijah had disappeared along with the light. Jesus stood alone. Jesus whispered, "Get up and do not be afraid."

Quietly they gathered their things and began the trek back down the mountain. As they journeyed Jesus admonished them, "Do not mention to anyone what you have seen, until the Son of Man has been raised from the dead."

More thoughts raced through Peter's head, *Yep, just when I think I found the answer to my questions I find myself with new questions! I think this event has topped everything else so far. What does it all mean?* (Matt 17:1-9).

Jesus said that we will be doing even greater things than He did. So, how does this story fit into what Jesus said? Before they went up to the mountain, clearly Jesus' words were connected to the meeting between Himself, Moses and Elijah. He said, "There are some of those standing here who will not taste death before they see the kingdom of God". So the kingdom is a *now* event, not a future event. The kingdom came before Peter, James and John died. So what is the connection?

The kingdom Jesus spoke about is the kingdom of heaven. He said His kingdom is "at hand" or it is right in front of your face. Jesus gave us the mandate to establish this kingdom here on earth.

Moses and Elijah are not on earth, but are a part of heaven and Jesus actually stood talking to them. Like Jesus we too can see those in this realm with no separation when we live with our spirit eyes open. Eyes that see in the Spirit close the chasm between heaven and earth and open a door between the realms. As we learn to function in this realm we will then work in tandem with the "great cloud of witnesses". Hebrews 11:40 says that those who have gone on before us will not be complete without us. So then we can also say that we will not be complete without them.

It's time for mature sons of God to start using their spirit eyes which is a sign of their citizenship in the kingdom of heaven. Jesus gave the mandate to, "Go into all the world preaching the good news to every person. And these attesting signs will accompany those who believe; in My name they will drive out demons; they will speak in new languages; they will pick up serpents and if they drink anything deadly, it will not hurt them; they will lay their hands on the sick and they will get well." (Mark 16:15).

To the degree we move in the seen, the bigger we can become deceived. So to avoid deception from the things of the world we need to open our spirit eyes to clearly see how God sees.

As we lay down our limited sight we then can begin to truly establish God's kingdom here on earth.

Jesus in Others

Most of us are aware when God is at work within us. We recognize the stirring of the Holy Spirit in some degree or other. Without it we would not have known our need for a Savior. After coming to believe and trust in Him our goal is to be formed into His image. Most of us desire to become more like Jesus.

But, how often do we get completely engulfed in what Jesus is doing in us then we miss what God is doing in others? Or could I also say, do we miss the Jesus in others because we are focused on their lack? Either way we fail to see the Jesus in one another which can lead us into either criticism or distrust; maybe both? Whichever, it keeps the body of Christ isolated from one another.

How does God see others? He sees them covered in the blood of Jesus; already perfected in Him. How often do we see the blood covering of Jesus upon others? If that could be the only thing we saw then we would not see the imperfections. Instead we pull out the measuring stick to measure everyone according to ourselves. We compare ourselves: Does their revelation measure up to the revelation God has given me? How do they compare to how I do things? The measuring often comes when we think they have fallen short of the wonders of our belief. The scripture states that we are unwise to compare ourselves with others (2 Cor 10:12) or compare them to ourselves. After all God shows no partiality towards people. (Eph 6:9; Rom 2:11). He doesn't measure one person any greater or lesser than the other. God takes it a step further and doesn't even see male or female. (Gal 3:28). So then why do we measure when we need to instead see Jesus in one another as God does?

Kate leaned in close as she excitedly shared, "The revelation was so powerful! God showed me that all my sin's were completely done away with and I am totally sinless! There is nothing I have to do but accept what Jesus did for me!" Her eyes gleamed with excitement.

While she was talking my mind raced with things God had shown me. I couldn't wait for her to finish so I could share what I knew.

I opened my mouth when the pause came, "Uh…", but then she continued to gush, "I have spent my whole life worried that I was doing something wrong! Whatever I did seemed to point towards what I should be doing for

God…always more I needed to do to be a better Christian! There is absolutely nothing I can do to gain His love or to obtain His pleasure!"

Finally I barged in sharing my thoughts, "I know! Isn't it awesome! We are so involved in doing things for Jesus that we miss living in the freedom He won for us. One thing God has been showing me is that we have relied on our "trainer," the law, to keep us from sinning which actually keeps us focused on sin. The scripture says that, "Grace trains us to reject all ungodliness and worldly desires, to live discreet upright lives in this present world." (Titus 2:11-12). We as a body of believers haven't learned to govern our soul man because it has ruled our lives through our works. If we don't learn to govern….".

"No! Did you hear what you said?" she sliced through my words. "We 'have' to learn? That is works. There is nothing we can do!"

"Now hear what I'm saying! If we don't learn to govern our inner life then we will not be able to govern the world around us," I countered.

Frustration brimmed as her words barely waited for me to finish, "We are totally free from sin! There is nothing else we need to do! My sin nature is dealt with. There is nothing else we need to do but live in Christ!"

I patiently stated, "There are still things that our fleshly nature does that haven't come into alignment with that truth. There is so much….".

"You're saying there is something we have to 'do'," she said as she leaned in closer.

Frustration began to rise in me because she kept cutting in and didn't seem to hear what I said. I continued on anyway, "I know that Jesus did everything for us and we are not sinners anymore, but because our soul has been the one in charge of our lives we have to bring it into alignment with the spirit man. We are being formed into Christ's image; taking off the old and putting on the new." Kate kept trying to talk over me but I kept talking, "We have to learn to walk in the new by denying our soul its place of dominion in our lives. Adam was created to have dominion over all the earth and he lost that dominion when he did things his way instead of God's way. When the second Adam came he governed His soul and did not give in to the lie of the enemy and He overcame by putting His and our flesh to death on the cross. Then He commissioned us to go into the entire world and cover it with His kingdom and rule as sons who are led by the Spirit not by the soul. We were created to govern. You govern your soul through the grace of the new man."

Impatience laced her words, "There is nothing we have to do! It's already done for us!"

I fell silent. She wasn't hearing what I was saying because she was so wrapped up in the revelation she had been given. What she was saying was very true but she couldn't receive anything beyond her own understanding. She was missing something further that God wanted to give her. What I was saying didn't lineup with her revelation so she dismissed it as wrong. How many times have most of us done this? I know I have.

Of course, I wasn't completely without wrong. While she was sharing about her revelation I found myself putting most of my attention on what I was going to say in response. I was thinking more about what I believed instead of being attentive to what God might want to reveal to me through her. Could it be I was wise in my own eyes - believing I was the only one with true revelation? Sad to say too many of us live in that arena too often!

Jesus will never give one person or group His full revelation. It isn't about an *either this thought or that thought* from each other but it is all about my thought *plus* your thought. So if we don't openly listen to what others are hearing from God we will only have a piece of the picture. I'm not saying everything you hear will be totally true, but there could be an aspect hidden within which will lead you into greater revelation. We need to trust that Jesus is actively speaking to others as much as He is to us. What if they are holding a key to what God has been longing to give you? God is calling us into unity and it begins by laying down our ideas knowing that not a single one of us has all the answers.

Most of the church rejected Martin Luther when he began to preach about justification. It didn't line up with their present theology so they fought against it because they thought they were right. But yet, today most of the church world accepts this concept into their theology without question. So what if some new thought, that doesn't line up with our present belief, is the next revelation that will launch the church into a greater alignment with heaven and our purpose on earth? So maybe we shouldn't be so quick to condemn something we don't understand.

We are to come together in Christ Jesus as the "Chief Cornerstone," (1 Peter 2:6) "living stones being built into a spiritual house," (1 Peter 2:4,5) not a fleshly house full of our own isolated understanding. We cannot become a complete house without the other stones. It is through the Spirit of God, not the flesh, "we are built up as a dwelling place of God." (Eph 2:22). We are being constructed; we are in process, to hold God's presence. As individuals we each hold the fullness of God within us. But it is only as we, the living stones, come together in unity that we will carry the embodiment of Him together. Each one of us contains a unique expression of God. As we come together it releases all of God into the earth. We become one body, Christ's body.

One thing that we often fail to realize is that what we are seeing or believing is a limited perspective. Each one of us can only see in part. We all have different angles of sight and there are things we do miss.

The scene was full of chaos where a two car collision had occurred in the middle of a busy residential area. One car was a black Toyota with the driver's side now shoved further into the car. The second car was a red Corvette nuzzled deep behind the driver's side of the black car. Grey steam rose in puffs from the smashed front-end of the red car with a trail of liquid rolling down the pavement from beneath it.

Neighbors were yanking at the black passenger door yelling at the man sitting motionless behind the wheel, "Sir, are you alright? We'll get you out."

A crowd was forming around the cars as the traffic came to a complete halt. With sirens blaring two police cars screeched to a stop as they vaulted from their car. From behind the wheel of the red car a woman was shoving at the door swearing as she tried to open it. Her blonde hair hung wildly in her face. One of the officer's ran to assist the woman with the door, "Ma'am! I've got it! Are your hurt?"

"Get me out of here!", she screamed.

"Stay calm….we'll get you out!" the officer yelled back.

The screech of metal shot through the air as the door flew open with the woman spilling out after it.

Another officer stepped over a cocker spaniel that lay motionless in the middle of the scene while reaching into the black car checking for the man's pulse. A trickle of blood was running down the man's face, "Sir, can you hear me?" he said as he touched the victim's face. The man's eyes fluttered open, "There you are!!" the officer yelled in delight.

A neighbor had made his way through the passenger side of the black car while he whispered to the man, "We'll have you out of here in no time. It'll be okay."

The man frantically began flailing his arms as he yelled, "The dog! The dog!"

"Don't worry about the dog right now, sir," the officer calmly stated, "We're here to help you." He knew the dog was dead, but they would deal with that later.

The man began to weep hysterically while the intermittent words spilled out, "The…the…dog! The dog!"

The neighbor said, "Sir, calm down! It will be okay! We're getting you out."

Soon the ambulance arrived with medical help for the victims. Having removed the man from his car they determined there were no life threatening injuries. As the man lay on a stretcher and the woman sat in the van, an officer questioned each one about the accident. At the same time other officers questioned some of the bystanders to see what they witnessed. As with most incidents everyone had a different view of what happened

Here is what they told the police officers:

Report from the woman in the red car: *"Before I entered the street I stopped for the black car to pass. As I was pulling out the car suddenly swerved into the lane closest to me stopping all of a sudden. He narrowly missed a cocker spaniel lying in the road. He stopped so quick that I plowed into him! I thought he was going to keep going. I can still see the shocked look on his face as I hit him."*

Report from a neighbor: *"I had just come out of the house to check my mail. I saw the black car passing by and then the red car didn't stop and ran right into him."*

Report from a bystander: *"My eyes were admiring the classy red corvette when I saw it stop for the black car. Then it headed out onto the road. The black car, instead of driving on, suddenly swerved and came to a complete stop in front of the red car. From out of nowhere this dog was in the road and he got tapped by the black car. The dog must have run across the road. Then the red car hit the black car."*

Report from the man in the black car: *"I was driving along with my dog in my lap. He started barking at a squirrel on the sidewalk. In a split second he jumped through the car window so I slammed on my brakes. I must have accidently pulled on the wheel making me go into the other lane. The last thing I remember is seeing this blonde woman in a red car plowing into me."*

No one person saw everything that happened. Each one had a little different story. It took the observation of all the people for the officer's to get the full picture of the accident. So it is with us in the body of Christ. We are all looking in on God's plan from different angles. Everyone is important in what God is doing; we all have a different view.

As we learn to trust the Jesus in one another we will begin to actually come together in true unity; the kind of unity God intends in His people. The unity God is releasing upon His people isn't about your belief or my belief. It's not about who's right or who's wrong. It is about the unity of sons who are all led by the Spirit alone. It is a harmony that will usher in the kingdom of God, releasing it into the earth where we will reconcile the world back to Him.

It is a time for each of us to lay down the false idea that we are the only one God speaks to. As we go lower we will begin to embrace all that God has poured into others.

Free to Be

Our judgments, criticisms and religious works prevents us to be free in who God intends us to be. It blocks us from freely living in our unique identity God gave us.

Jesus has completely set us free (John 8:32) from the things that keep us from functioning in our true identity and purpose. So if the Son has certainly liberated you, then you will be unrestrained - really! (John 8:36). Jesus removed all the restraints of performance that holds each of us in bondage to the flesh; which keeps us from our identity as spirit beings. So why aren't we living as liberated sons? Why do we also bind our brethren from living as free? Mostly because we do not realize to what degree we are in bondage to our flesh. Jesus overcame by not pleasing Himself but only pleasing the Father. He lived as a man led by the Spirit not as a man ruled by His flesh.

When we begin to live according to the Spirit we then are free to engage in all that Jesus restored back to us. Living under the rule of the spirit gives us liberty because, "He whom the Son sets free is free indeed." (2 Cor 3:17). I like saying, "He whom the Son sets free is free 'from deeds'." We are liberated from oppressive restrictions and a controlling religious system. We are liberated…set free! This freedom is realized when we "…look carefully into the law of liberty" (James 1:25) where we become what we behold. We need to keep the things of the Spirit in our sight at all times. Under God's government He gives us His grace that teaches us to live in that freedom.

This freedom is realized in the new covenant God has made with His people. In that new covenant, through the testimony of Holy Spirit, God said, "I will imprint My laws upon their hearts, and I will inscribe them on their minds" (Jer 31:31-34; Heb 8: 10,11; Heb 10: 15,16). We now have a new covenantal law imprinted upon our hearts where we don't need anyone to teach us, even though we still have teachers, because Holy Spirit guides us into all Truth. (John 16:13). There is nothing like being taught by the Spirit instead of trying to obtain it through our own effort or our own wisdom. We all have the ability to hear from God; His law is written on every believer's heart. But yet God will only give each of us a part of His truth so we will find it together. We need to be free to hear Holy Spirit for ourselves, but also embrace what God is saying to others.

But yet sadly many people are discouraged from hearing for themselves for fear of being led into false doctrine. Too often, unknowingly, it is implied that we need leaders to hear for us. Fear of failing to correctly hear Holy Spirit has paralyzed much of the church today. At times when the few brave do listen for themselves they are pushed away as "out of line" radicals. This concept has bound and kept the body of Christ from functioning in their true identity as spiritual beings; as sons with a direct line to their Father. After all Jesus did remove the hostile dividing wall between us and the Father. (Eph 2:14).

Too often, because we fear deception, we think we have to have others hear God for us. So we seek out pastors or leaders, who must be more spiritual, so we can gain God's attention before He will assist us in our need.

The invitation was given for anyone who needed prayer to come forward. This was how we ended our church meeting…most of the time. People began to trickle forward; the prayer team was ready and in position.

As I stood waiting with the ministry team, Marty made a beeline for me. I thought, *He's going to have the same prayer request he's had for the last ten years!* I felt sorry for him and he never seemed to move beyond his problem. It was like he had a deaf ear to all the good prayer sessions over the years. I was getting to the point I didn't want to pray for him anymore…sad to say.

"Hello Marty! What do you need prayer for this morning?" I asked as I took him by the hand. For his thirty-one years he had experienced a lot of negative things. His black hair and clothes had that slept in look. He was such a sweet young man and my heart ached for him. Since becoming a Christian, life did get better for him in many ways, but he seemed to have a hard time maintaining the freedom. For weeks he would be better, but then he would get slammed back down into the old patterns of depression.

As he was telling me about his prayer need, I was asking Holy Spirit, "What more can be said to this young man? Give me a key to help him maintain his freedom." Oddly enough I heard Holy Spirit whisper, "Don't pray for him. It is time he begins to come into maturity and seek me on his own. He must learn to govern his thoughts and choose to not go down the familiar road." Okay! I had never told anyone coming for prayer that I would not pray for them! This was different.

Marty was staring at me ready for my prayer. I slowly began, "Marty how long have you been coming up for us to pray for you? About ten years, right?" He nodded his head in confirmation. I carefully continued, "I have been asking God, after all the prayers you have received, why you still need to be prayed for over the same issues again and again. I believe there is something deep down in your belief system that other people's prayers are more powerful than yours. Even after all your encounters with God, after all the many great things God has taught you, you still seem to struggle with the same old things over and over. It's time to begin to learn how to function as a mature son of God that has learned to govern his own thoughts and choices. You can choose what thoughts to keep or throw out. When you allow your thoughts to run amuck, then you end back in depression and negative thoughts. I can pray for you forever, but you will still get back into depression. You must learn to take authority over the path your thoughts travel down. It is time you realize your prayers are just as powerful as mine or anyone else's. So, surprisingly enough, I am not going to pray for you today."

Shock flushed across his face as his blank gaze bore into my eyes. His mouth opened briefly as if to say something, then he closed it tight.

"You have the fullness of Jesus living in you! You, in Him, have the ability to maintain your freedom from depression. What happens is that you keep turning your thoughts and attention onto the negative things in your life. Philippians 1:28 says, "Do not be frightened or intimidated in anything by your opponents and adversaries, for such will be a clear sign to them of [their impending] destruction, but [a sure token and evidence] of your deliverance and salvation, and that from God." When you do not give attention to the storm around you then it is a clear sign of your enemies defeat and a sign of your victory. Turn your attention away from the negative thoughts and choices and through Jesus it will bring you victory. You have to learn to take authority over your thoughts. I believe this is a step to maintain your freedom."

The blank stare had changed into relief. He was nodding in agreement as I continued, "I am going to have you pray for yourself and take authority over the depression."

He bowed his head as he whispered, "I didn't realize…I thought other people's prayers were more powerful than mine. Wow! Okay let's do this!"

After he prayed the depression completely left. Tears were running down his face as he joyously hugged me. That was one of the most fun prayer sessions I have had; leading someone into the reality of the power of the Holy Spirit living in them, and that they have the power to govern their inner life. He learned that day the importance of coming into agreement with the freedom that Jesus had already given him and what kept him from embracing that truth. Through learning to govern his soul he was led into freedom from a soul ruled life. Also, the tools he was given he could apply at anytime without the need to run to someone else to pray for him.

The earth is groaning for true sons of God to be manifest so it can be set free from its bondage. Groans are heard from the earth for restored sons to be revealed in their original role as spiritual dads, governors, overseers, and sons who hear the voice of their Father just as Adam did before the fall. The door into hearing Holy Spirit comes through laying down our way and living in Christ Jesus as a simple carefree child.

Sunlight filtered through the open window adorned by a windblown curtain. Its beam lit up the coloring book and the chubby little hand wildly running the colored marker across the page. It was as if the lines of the printed figure were invisible to the green marks beginning to cover the page.

The blonde shoulder length hair dangled chaotically around the furiously moving hand of the toddler lying over the coloring book. Quickly sitting up, the child pushed her hair back with her fingers, unaware of the green mark she had just put across her forehead. Gripping the coloring book with her color streaked hands she pulled it close to her face examining the masterpiece.

As Jennifer walked into the living room she could see her daughter, Amy, on the floor looking at her coloring book. It was hard to believe she was already over two and half years old. Her heart warmed as she was met with a chubby cheeked smile sporting green and blue marks smudged across the lips.

"Mommy! Looky what I did!" Amy squealed. Jumping up, Amy teetered wildly while flinging her artwork into Jennifer's hands to show her the colorful work of art.

"Amy! This is so pretty. There are so many colors!" Jennifer said as she examined the picture. It was a picture of a man who now had blue arms, purple legs and a green face. "So this man has a green face. How many people do you know with green faces?"

A solemn look came across Amy's face as she whispered, "I like green, it's pretty."

"Green is a beautiful, bright color! He looks good with a green face!" Jennifer said as she looked into her daughter's big blue eyes.

Amy pulled away and began to dance around the room singing, "Green makes me happy! I like green!" A plaid pink and blue skirt flared with each twirled swoop. Clinging tightly to her upper body was last year's shirt of red and purple flowers which was turned wrong-side out with its tag brushing her chin. Jennifer watched the little feet bouncing up and down with one bare foot and the other clad with a red sock. Giggling Amy fell to the floor rolling into a sprawled position looking at the ceiling smiling.

There wasn't much that could make Amy sad; she always had a joyous outlook. When she had determinedly learned to dress herself Jennifer was always amazed at what she came out of her room wearing for the moment. Most days she changed a number of times before the day was out. Life was carefree and fun!

To Amy it didn't matter what anyone thought of her; she was herself. No one had yet taught her the "rules" of being concerned of others opinion of her. Amy didn't worry about her mismatched clothes, the ink marks smudged across her face or how she had colored outside the lines. Amy was free in who she was; she was free to be.

"Whoever accordingly brings themselves low as this little child, the same is the greatest in the kingdom of heaven." (Matt 18:4). The way up is down. Our adult religious ways are framed in our own wisdom and with rules to guide us. This is why we miss the greatest adventure we could be living. We've become wise in our own eyes. The carefree joy like a little child has been long ago forgotten. Joy and freedom get lost in the fleshly busyness of man.

One fictional character that displays freedom and joy is the story of Peter Pan. He didn't want to grow up. I think deep down inside he knew that he would lose the simple joyful imagination that made him free to explore new realms.

I love the ending words of the song, "You Can Fly" from the Disney movie Peter Pan: "Think of all the joy you'll find when you leave the world behind and bid your cares goodbye. You can fly! You can fly! You can fly!"

Becoming a little child happens when we are able to leave the cares of a fleshly world behind; worry and anxiety; leaving all fear of failure or the opinions of man behind. It happens when we go lower as a little child leaving all the works and our self-wisdom in the rear view mirror to fly in the Spirit as true sons of God whose citizenship is heaven.

The way to fly up in the spirit is to go down away from the flesh! You can fly! You can fly!

ABOUT THE AUTHOR

Sheila Parnell is a speaker and teacher who draws out the destiny and identity in the body of Christ. Through her ministry many come into a fresh new perspective of themselves in relation to their Father, God. She loves to release a true joy that ushers people into laughter and new hope.

Through her writing and speaking she ministers to people on a personal level that leads them to become mature sons of God who are free to be led by Holy Spirit. Her goal is to create insightful, relevant teachings that anyone can activate in their everyday life and to deepen their walk with God.

Sheila was formerly The Dalles Aglow President and Aglow Area Team Leader. During this time she and her husband, Phil, served as Directors of The Dalles River Gate Healing Rooms.

In 2009 she resigned from the Aglow Area Team and became the Healing Rooms Regional Assistant Director, IAHR. In 2013 as she was returning from a trip in Africa Sheila heard God whisper, "It is time to begin focusing on the ministry I have given to you and your husband." In January 2014 she stepped down from The Healing Rooms to give her full attention to Benchmark Ministries and to her writing.

Sheila and her husband Phil has been married for 42 years. They have 4 grown children and 11 grandchildren. The Dalles, Oregon is their place of residence.

Sheila Parnell contact:

Benchmark Ministries
PO Box 1185
The Dalles, Oregon 97058

www.benchmarkmin.org
www.sheilaparnell.net
www.facebook.com/SheilaKParnell